FASCINATING
BIBLE
FACTS

PEOPLE, PLACES & EVENTS

PUBLICATIONS INTERNATIONAL, LTD.

Picture credits:

Front cover: **SuperStock**

Back cover: **The Crosiers**

Bible Pictures: 11, 13, 23, 28, 31, 39, 49, 51, 63, 125, 140, 151, 158, 163, 165,
200, 201, 223, 228, 237, 242, 247, 248, 253, 267, 281, 286, 288, 292, 295, 297,
313, 316, 321, 343, 367; **Werner Braun:** 3, 97, 101, 179, 225, 323, 325, 327,
332, 355, 360, 363, 368, 373; **Cambridge University Press:** 69; **The Dore
Bible Illustrations/Dover Publications, Inc. 1974:** 18, 25, 37, 42, 47, 57,
60, 83, 113, 121, 129, 131, 136, 138, 142, 160, 181, 187, 189, 194, 197, 215,
218, 221, 245, 251, 255, 257, 260, 270, 272, 274, 277, 284, 299, 309, 318; **FPG
International:** 349; David Bartruff: 73; Th.D.A. de Lange: 77; Keystone View
Co.: 85; Richard T. Nowitz: 117; Len Rue, Jr./Leonard Rue Enterprises: 154;
Paul M. Schrock Photos: 265; **NASA:** 7, 191; **The New Testament/Dover
Publications, Inc. 1986:** 55, 65, 88, 146, 209, 212, 235, 239, 303, 306, 337;
Richard T. Nowitz: 330, 353; **Richard & Varda Nowitz:** 169, 174, 233;
Zev Radovan: 93, 104, 109, 205, 263; **Lorie Robare:** 9, 91; **SuperStock:**
183, 135.

❧ CONTENTS ❧

T hough many of the stories in the Bible are well known, much of the history and background may not be as well known. How do we make the Bible come alive—make it real? *Fascinating Bible Facts* fills in the background and gives details about the people, places, and cultures of biblical times. Find out about the lives of kings and queens, emperors and warriors, and heroes and villains. These were people who breathed, ate, slept, worried, cried, and rejoiced.

To give you the best information possible, the author has chosen to quote from many sources, including the Revised Standard Version, New Revised Standard Version, King James Version, New King James Version, New American Bible, New International Version, New American Standard Version, New Jewish Publication Society Version, and the author has translated directly from the Hebrew. Most quotations of ancient Middle Eastern manuscripts are from *Ancient Near Eastern Texts Relating to the Old Testament,* by J. B. Pritchard; the author translated the remainder.

So explore the biblical world in *Fascinating Bible Facts.* Deepen your understanding and increase your knowledge as you explore page after page!

Reading the Torah at the Western Wall.

Genesis: Book of Origins

The Bible's first book deals with origins, naturally enough. It tells the stories of the creation of the world and humanity. It also tells about the introduction of evil into the world. Then the book focuses upon the life of Abraham's family, the father of the Jews, through whom God established his special plans for the human race.

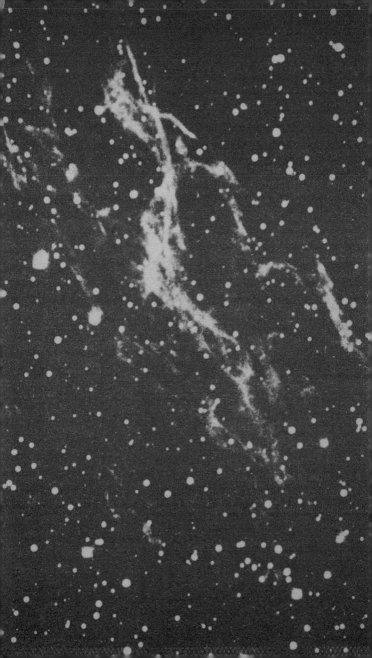

⚛ ABOUT THE BIBLE ⚛

When Was Adam Created?

In 1650, Archbishop James Ussher calculated that the world was created in 4004 B.C. A few years later, John Lightfoot calculated that Adam was created on October 23 at 9:00 a.m. One scholar, quoted in *The Christian View of Science and Scripture,* commented dryly that "Closer than this, as a cautious scholar, the Vice-Chancellor of Cambridge University did not venture to commit himself."

Reading Backward

Often in Hebrew, words are placed out of their natural order to produce a special impact or effect. One dramatic example is in Genesis 6:9, in the phrase "Noah walked with God." Noah is found at the end of the sentence; when it is read backward, the name Enoch is revealed. Enoch was also a man who "walked with God" (Genesis 5:24).

Hebrew Shorthand

Rabbis interpreted some words in the Hebrew Bible as actually standing for entire phrases. That is, they argued that each letter of certain words represented a different word of a phrase. The first word of the Bible, *Br'shyt* ("in the beginning"), was said to represent several different phrases, one of which was "in the beginning God saw that Israel would accept the Torah."

Exodus: Birth of a Nation

Exodus tells the stories of Israel's captivity in Egypt and how Moses freed his people. The Ten Commandments were given on Mount Sinai, as well as details of the great Covenant Code of Laws and detailed instructions for the Tabernacle—the tent where God dwelled.

The Parting of the Waters

Three times the Bible mentions waters being miraculously parted. The Red Sea parted when Israel, led by Moses, was fleeing the Egyptians and needed to cross. The Jordan River parted twice, first when the Israelites under Joshua needed to cross it in order to enter the promised land. The second time the Jordan River parted was when the prophets Elijah and Elisha needed to cross.

Who Was El Shaddai?

One of God's titles was *El Shaddai,* which is usually translated as "God Almighty." God told Moses that he had appeared to Abraham, Isaac, and Jacob as El Shaddai, but that he did not reveal to them the full implications of his personal name, Yahweh (Exodus 6:3).

God's name in Hebrew

"I AM WHO I AM"

When Moses asked God what his name was, God responded with this cryptic phrase: "I am who I am" (Exodus 3:14). These words in Hebrew are related to God's personal name, Yahweh. God may have been revealing something profound about himself, or he also may have been reminding Moses of his earlier promise that "I will be with you" (verse 12).

God's Personal Name

Just as the Canaanite high god's personal name was Baal, the Mesopotamian high god's name was Marduk, or the Egyptian high god's name was Ra, so the Israelites' God had a personal name, Yahweh. Its exact meaning is debated; it either means "he creates" or "he is (with his people)."

Don't Say That Name!

The personal name of God (written as Y-H-W-H) was so holy to the Jews that they eventually stopped pronouncing it because they felt unworthy. When they encountered this name in the Bible while reading aloud, they substituted one of God's titles, *adonay* ("the Lord"). In most English Bibles today, God's personal name is written in small capital letters as "the LORD".

Who Was Jehovah?

Jehovah was the rendering of God's personal name that arose when the consonants of his name were combined with the vowels of its substitute in oral reading (Y-H-W-H and adonay): Yahowah. This mixed-up form was never heard in the Jewish synagogue, but entered the common English language by the King James Bible.

Leviticus: Instructions for Holy Living

This book contains instructions for the Levites—the clergy for whom the book is named—and others concerning holiness. Many laws relate to animal sacrifices, but every law is related in one way or another to the need for personal holiness and blamelessness in relationship with God and with others. It contains the famous injunction about loving one's neighbor as oneself (Leviticus 19:18).

The Israelites and the Ark of the Covenant

Numbers: Censuses, Laws, and Journeys

The Book of Numbers is about preparations for Israel to enter the land of Canaan. The people are numbered, more instructions are given, and the starts and stops of their journey to the promised land are detailed, including the 38 years of wandering in the wilderness.

An Ancient Folk Song

Folk songs around the world arise from everyday life, and even the Bible records some. One was sung to commemorate a well:

"Spring up, O well—sing to it—the well which the chieftains dug, which the nobles of the people started with maces, with their own staffs" (Numbers 21:17,18).

Hidden Meanings in the Numbers

In later Jewish literature, much weight was given to secret meanings hidden in the numerical values of words. In Hebrew, numbers are written using the Hebrew alphabet. Thus, in Genesis 14:14, where Abraham had 318 servants, this is seen as a hidden reference to Eliezer (the servant of Abraham, mentioned in Genesis 15:2), because 318 is the numerical value of the word Eliezer. Also, the numerical value of both the words wine and secret is 70; this led to the saying "when wine enters, secrets are out."

A Real Numbers Game

The finding of hidden meanings in numbers was called gematria, and it was often used to entertain and exhort, rather than to make serious claims about biblical meanings. The four consonants of God's name (Y-H-W-H) have numerical values as follows: 10, 5, 6, 5. The sum of their squares is 186, which is the numerical value of M-Q-W-M, which means "place." This reminded the rabbis that God is omnipresent (in every place).

"Do Not Muzzle An Ox"

The Law of Moses made provision for humane treatment of animals when it stated "You shall not muzzle an ox when it treads out the grain" (Deuteronomy 25:4). The Apostle Paul saw a greater concern in that law. He used it as an allegory representing God's ministers, by which he urged the churches to generously support the clergy.

The Israelites wander in the wilderness.

Deuteronomy: Second Law

The book's title means second law, and it repeats and adds to many of the laws found in Exodus, Leviticus, and Numbers. The laws are framed by a series of Moses' last addresses to the people of

Israel, in which he reviews God's gracious dealings with them in the wilderness. Moses urges the people to live faithful lives in their new land, Canaan.

The Ten Commandments

The Ten Commandments form the heart of the Old Testament law. They are the universal moral principles that the rest of the law expands upon in specific detail. They are important in the Old Testament itself. They are listed twice (Exodus 20, Deuteronomy 5), and they are referred to as "the ten words" (Exodus 34:28; Deuteronomy 4:13, 10:4).

The 613 Commandments

The Jewish rabbis counted 613 separate commandments in the Law of Moses. Of those, 365 of them (one for each day of the year) were stated negatively, and 248 positively. The first two of the Ten Commandments came directly from God, and 611 commandments were said to have been given through Moses. Interestingly enough, the number 611 is the numerical value of the word Torah, which means "law," "commandment," or "instruction."

The Golden Rule I

Many people know that Jesus summarized the entire Law of Moses by saying that "You shall love the Lord your God with all your heart, soul, and mind, and love your neighbor as yourself" (Matthew 22:37–40). What many don't realize is that Jesus was only quoting the Old Testament. The first command is found in Deuteronomy 6:5 and the second in Leviticus 19:18.

The Golden Rule II

Almost every major religion has a statement similar to Jesus' about loving one's neighbor. The great Jewish rabbi Hillel, who lived before Christ, was asked by a skeptic to teach him the entire Torah while standing on one leg. Hillel's response was, "What is hateful to yourself do not do to another. This is the whole Torah; go and study it; the rest is commentary."

Symbolic Numbers

Many numbers had symbolic value in the Bible. The number one symbolized God's unity. Three came to symbolize the Trinity. Seven was a number of completion and perfection, since God rested on the seventh day of creation. Twelve symbolized the months of the year, the tribes of Israel, and the number of apostles. Forty days or years was a common time frame in which events unfolded.

Large Symbolic Numbers

Many significant numbers were multiples of smaller symbolic numbers. Seventy was a large number of completion. The number 666 is the mark of the beast in Revelation 13:18, a symbol of the antichrist. The number 1,000 symbolized something indefinitely large. The number 144,000 is the number of saints sealed up to God in Revelation 7:4 and 14:1.

Joshua: Book of the Land

This book focuses entirely on the land of Canaan and the Israelites' possession of it as the fulfillment of God's promise to Abraham. Moses' successor, Joshua, led Israel into the land, did battle with the Canaanites at Jericho and elsewhere, and portioned out the land to the 12 tribes of Israel.

Hallelu–Yah!

The word *hallelujah* is Hebrew for "praise the Lord." It contains a shortened form of God's name: Yah (for Yahweh). Many biblical characters' names end similarly: Hezekiah is *chizqi-yah* "Yahweh is my strength," and Isaiah is *yesha-yahu* "Yahweh saves."

Elohim: God or gods?

Elohim is the Hebrew word for "God" and it also is the word for (foreign) "gods." It is a grammatically plural word (it means gods), but when it refers to God, it takes a singular verb. This plural form of the word for one God is sometimes called the plural of majesty. It is almost as if God's attributes are so many and he is so great that no mere singular noun can do him justice.

Judges: Time of Turmoil

The book of Israel's judges tells a story of a repeated cycle of the nation's sin, enslavement, and deliverance by warrior-judges. The cycle spirals downward, however, and by the end of the book things are so bad that the author despairingly says, "in those days there was no king in Israel; everyone did what was right in their own eyes."

A Deadly Climax

Hebrew poetry can be very dramatic. The poetic description of Sisera's (the Canaanite general) death, whom Jael killed with a tent peg through his temple, shows an awful death struggle:
"Between her feet he sank, he fell, he lay,
Between her feet he sank, he fell.
Where he sank, there he fell,
Dead" (Judges 5:27).

The Lion and the Bees

Riddles were common in the biblical world. Their intent was to puzzle the hearers. Only after the riddle was interpreted did its point become clear. A well-known riddle was Samson's: "Out of the eater came something to eat. Out of the strong came something sweet" (Judges 14:14). This referred to a lion he had killed and in whose carcass bees had made honey. Because the riddle was answered, Samson killed 30 Philistines with the jawbone of an ass.

Whatever in the World Is Onomatopoeia?!

This refers to words that sound like what they describe, such as "buzz" or "boom." An interesting Hebrew example refers to the "galloping, galloping" sounds of Canaanite war-horses in an Israelite victory song: "*daharote, daharote*" (Judges 5:22).

Ruth: A Love Story

The Book of Ruth is a literary masterpiece, a sparkling gem that tells a heartwarming story about a widowed woman (Naomi) and her daughter-in-law (Ruth) for whom things finally work out in the end. Ruth marries Boaz, who provides for them both. The family tree at the book's end connects Ruth with Abraham and shows her to be David's great-grandmother.

Ruth gathers grain from Boaz's field.

Ruth: Exemplar of the Virtuous Woman

In the Hebrew Bible, the Book of Ruth immediately follows the Book of Proverbs (rather than the Book of Judges, as it does in the Christian canon). This is probably because Proverbs ends with the great poem about the many virtues of a godly woman (Proverbs 31:10–31). The Book of Ruth follows because Ruth is a perfect example of just such a woman.

1 and 2 Samuel: King David's Story

These books tell of the introduction of kingship in Israel under the prophet Samuel. Israel's first king, Saul, was disqualified, and David became king. Three-quarters of the book is devoted to David's rise to power and to his reign. God promised David an unbroken line of successors on the throne of the kingdom.

Medieval Copyists

During the Middle Ages, Jewish scribes and Christian monks kept the Scriptures alive by laboriously copying them over and over again by hand. Copying became a true art form. Scribes and monks, for example, used elaborate calligraphy and different-colored inks in their manuscripts. They also drew tiny, beautifully detailed pictures in the margins and at the beginning of chapters.

Copyists' Misteaks (sic)

Scholars who believe the Bible was originally written without any errors do not argue that there were no mistakes in its copying. As manuscripts were copied again and again by hand over many centuries, many misspellings, additions, and omissions occurred. Fortunately, enough biblical manuscripts survive so scholars can compare them and confidently judge what the original texts say.

Was Saul An Infant King?

A famous text where copying errors have crept in is in 1 Samuel 13:1. The Hebrew literally reads "Saul was one year old when he became king, and he reigned two years over Israel." Since we know that Saul became king as an adult and that he reigned for more than two years, this indicates that at least two numbers were missed by an ancient copyist.

Dueling Versions?

Bible translators must resort to educated guesses in those rare instances where the texts we have are unintelligible. In 1 Samuel 13:1, the King James Version reads: "Saul reigned one year; and when he had reigned two years ...." The New American Standard Version reads "Saul was forty years old when he began to reign, and he reigned thirty-two years ...." The New International Version reads "Saul was thirty years old when he became king, and he reigned forty-two years ...."

1 and 2 Kings: The Kings of Israel and Judah

Under David's son Solomon, the nation began to crumble and eventually it split into two: northern Israel (ten tribes) and southern Judah (two tribes).

These books chronicle the fortunes of the two kingdoms. Israel had an unbroken succession of bad kings and Judah had the descendants of David and a mixture of good and bad kings. The books end with Israel annihilated and Judah under Babylonian captivity.

The Septuagint

The earliest Greek translation of the Hebrew Bible is called the Septuagint. Supposedly, 72 translators (representing six from each tribe of Israel) were convened in Alexandria, Egypt, about 250 B.C., but scholars today put its translation later, and taking place over a long period of time. This translation was needed because so many Jews throughout the Mediterranean world only spoke Greek.

Aramaic Targums

Aramaic was a sister language to Hebrew, and was used starting in the late Old Testament period. The earliest Aramaic translations of the Hebrew Bible were the Targums. These were oral paraphrases on each book, not exact translations, and they were laden with commentary and explanatory glosses. The earliest of these were committed to writing during the period between the composition of the last book of the Old Testament and the first book of the New Testament.

A Reverence for Scripture

In early Jewish custom, translation of the Hebrew Scriptures in the worship services could only be done orally, not read from a scroll. This probably was to preserve the distinctiveness and sacredness of the written Hebrew Scriptures. It is said of the great Rabbi Gamaliel, the Apostle Paul's teacher, that he rejected a written copy of the Aramaic Targum of Job and had it buried in a wall.

1 and 2 Chronicles: David's Kingdom

Fully half of these two books are copied word-for-word from 1 and 2 Samuel and 1 and 2 Kings, but the author presents a very different slant. He is only interested in the fortunes of David and the kingdom of Judah (which represented David's descendants), and he consistently evaluates the nation's fortunes in terms of its trust in God.

The Hebrew Bible: Different Numbering

Early references to the Hebrew Bible (the Old Testament) mentioned only 22 or 24 books in it, instead of 39, as found in Christian Bibles, even though their contents are identical. This is because books such as 1 and 2 Kings were counted as one, and the 12 minor prophets (Hosea through Malachi) were counted as one, called The Book of the Twelve.

The Hebrew Bible: Different Ordering

Even though it has the same books as the Christian Old Testament, the Hebrew Bible arranges its contents differently. It has three sections, called (in order) the Law, the Prophets, and the Writings. The Prophets include the historical books such as 1 and 2 Samuel along with the traditional prophets, such as Isaiah. The Writings include Psalms and

many other miscellaneous books, and it ends with
2 Chronicles.

Books That Defile the Hands

For Jewish rabbis, books that were given by divine
inspiration were ones that "defiled the hands" if
they were touched. This idea prevented irreverent
use of the Scriptures. If people had to wash their
hands every time they handled the Scriptures, they
would handle them carefully and reverently.

Solomon rebuilds the Temple.

Ezra and Nehemiah:
Books of Restoration

These books show the restoration of Judah after the
destruction of Jerusalem and the Israelites exile in

Babylon. The Temple was rebuilt and Ezra and Nehemiah returned from exile to Judah to start religious and political reforms, which included rebuilding the walls of the city.

Selective Genealogies

The Bible has many genealogies, listing generation after generation almost endlessly it seems at times. Sometimes these genealogies are not all-inclusive, however. Jesus is called "the son of David, the son of Abraham" (Matthew 1:1), when generations separated the three men. A list of Aaron's descendants in Ezra 7:1–5 omits six people who are found in the parallel list in 1 Chronicles 6:3–14.

Esther: God's Protection in Exile

The Book of Esther tells of the fortunes of a Jewish family who never returned from exile, but who flourished in a foreign land. Esther and her uncle Mordechai were favored and rose in the Persian court, despite strong opposition from their enemies, and they were able to avert a great slaughter of Jews.

God Hidden in Esther

Even though God is not mentioned directly in the Book of Esther, the Jewish rabbis did find his name in the book, hidden in an acrostic. The first letters of four succeeding Hebrew words at a crucial point in the book are the same four letters that form the basis for God's holy name: Y-H-W-H (Yahweh). The rabbis felt that God still maintained an unseen presence in the book.

Esther confronts Haman.

Esther: Book of Controversy

The Book of Esther has provoked strong reactions. Negatively, Martin Luther, the great Protestant reformer, wrote that "I am so hostile to this book [2 Maccabees] and to Esther that I could wish they did not exist at all." Positively, Maimonides, the great

Jewish rabbi, elevated it to near equality with the
Law of Moses, saying that the Law and Esther would
still stand after all other Scripture had perished.

Job: Questions About Innocent Suffering

The Book of Job is one of the world's classics on
the question of human suffering and divine justice.
Job, an innocent man who feared God, is put
through much suffering. Through this, Job
passionately questions God but he never abandons
belief in God. After a direct encounter with God,
Job's questions cease and his fortunes are fully
restored.

What Is Wisdom?

Wisdom in the biblical sense refers to knowing how
to live life well, in all its dimensions, including
relationships with God and with one's fellow human
beings. The three "wisdom" books in the Bible are
Job, Proverbs, and Ecclesiastes. The Book of
Proverbs begins by stating that "The fear of the
Lord is the beginning of knowledge; fools despise
wisdom and instruction" (Proverbs 1:7).

How Can Wisdom Be Acquired?

Job 28 contains a majestic poem reflecting on what
wisdom is and how it can be acquired. It states that
wisdom is not to be found in the deepest sea, nor
can it be bought for gold, nor can any animal or
human being know it on its own. Only "God
understands the way to it, and he knows its place"
(verse 23). God is the source of wisdom and he
reveals it to humans.

Psalms: Israel's Songs and Prayers

The 150 psalms in the Psalter formed a hymn book of sorts for Israel. These hymns cover the range of human emotion, from ecstatic joy to deepest despair. They have taught Jews and Christians how to sing and pray, and also conveyed truths about God and everyday faith and life.

"I've Told You a Million Times Not to Exaggerate!"

Hyperbole, or exaggeration, is a common poetic device in Hebrew. In describing his troubles, one psalmist says "I am sinking in deep slime…I have come into deep water, and the flood sweeps me away" (Psalm 69:1). It is comical to imagine the poet literally holding scroll and pen above the water as he sinks out of sight!

Two-in-One Psalms

Some psalms now separated in the Bible originally were part of one composition. Psalms 9 and 10 contain an acrostic poem that begins with the first letter of the Hebrew alphabet in Psalm 9:1 and ends in Psalm 10:17 with the last letter. Psalms 42 and 43 share a refrain, also showing a common origin.

Duplicate Psalms

Some psalms appear more than once in the Bible. David's song of praise when God delivered him from the hands of Saul appears as 2 Samuel 22 and also as Psalm 18. The psalm beginning "The fool says in his heart, 'There is no God,'" appears as both Psalm 14 and 53.

The Ark of the Covenant

Cut-and-Paste Psalms

Some psalms were composed in much the same way that modern church prayer books are, by stringing together different portions of Scripture to form new compositions. Psalm 108 is made up entirely of parts of Psalms 57 and 60, and the lengthy hymn of thanksgiving when the Ark reached Jerusalem found in 1 Chronicles 16 is composed of poetry found in three psalms: 96, 105, and 106.

Head for the Center

A well-written essay usually states its objective somewhere near the beginning. Some biblical psalms, however, make their main point halfway through. These psalms are so precisely constructed that you can count the number of Hebrew words in the psalm, divide by two, and find the psalm's most important thought precisely at the midpoint. Examples include Psalms 8, 23, 95, and 100.

Which Psalm Is It?

Protestant Bibles (which follow the Hebrew Bible's numbering system) number the psalms differently from many Roman Catholic and Orthodox Bibles (which follow the earliest Greek and Latin versions). In the latter, Psalms 9 and 10 were treated as one psalm. Thus, the numbering of Psalms 10 through 113 is off by one. After this, several other adjustments in how psalms are divided also affect the numbering. All Bibles end with 150 total psalms, however.

Psalms for a Pilgrimage

Fifteen consecutive psalms have the title "A Psalm of Ascents": Psalms 120 to 134. Rabbinic tradition states that there were 15 steps going up from the Women's Court in the Temple to the Israelites' Court, and that a psalm was composed for each. More likely, these psalms were composed for the pilgrimage up to Jerusalem, "the mountain of the Lord" (Isaiah 30:29).

Books Within the Psalter

The Book of Psalms is organized into five books, consisting of Psalms 1 to 41, 42 to 72, 73 to 89, 90 to 106, and 107 to 150. Each of these concludes with a short doxology, praising God, and the word amen. The Jewish Midrash (commentary) on the Psalms, written in the tenth century A.D., equates this division with that of the Pentateuch: "As Moses gave five books of laws to Israel, so David gave five books of Psalms to Israel."

Psalms Outside the Psalter

Besides the 150 psalms in the biblical Psalter, the Bible has many other psalms scattered throughout other books. Famous examples include psalms in Exodus 15 (Moses and Miriam's Song of the Sea), Deuteronomy 32 (Moses' song), Judges 5 (Deborah and Barak's victory song), 1 Samuel 2 (Hannah's song of praise), 2 Samuel 1 (David's lament), Jonah 2 (Jonah's prayer of thanksgiving), Habakkuk 3 (Habakkuk's song of praise), and Luke 1 (Mary's song of praise, called The Magnificat).

Psalm Titles

Many of the psalms (116 in all) have titles that were added in antiquity. Many attribute the psalm to a certain author (David, Asaph, sons of Korah), while many classify the psalm (as a prayer, a praise, a *maskil,* a *miktam,* a *shiggaion*). Some contain musical instructions ("For the choir director"), while others have historical notes ("A Psalm of David, when Nathan the prophet came to him after he went into Bathsheba").

The Annunciation

Name That Tune!

Many psalm titles contain musical instructions that
are not clear today. These include Psalm 6
("According to the Sheminith"), Psalm 22

("According to 'The Hind of the Dawn'"),
Psalm 45 ("According to 'Lilies'"), and Psalm 56
("According to 'The Dove on Far-Off
Terebinths'"). These probably refer to the titles of
specific tunes to be used with these psalms.

Biblical Acrostics

Highly structured Hebrew poetry found its most
specialized expression in the acrostic poem, where
each succeeding verse in the poem began with
succeeding letters of the Hebrew alphabet, 22 in all.
Psalms 25, 34, 37, 111, 112, 119, and 145 are all
examples of this. The poem extolling the virtues of
a godly woman in Proverbs 31:10–31 is also an
acrostic.

Proverbs: Practical Wisdom

This book is one of the most practical books in the
Bible, with its common-sense approach to life. This
is captured in hundreds of short, pithy sayings
(proverbs) about how to live life well, in all its
dimensions, with God and our neighbors.

Solomon: A Real Numbers Cruncher

The Book of Proverbs contains many proverbs of
Solomon, including one section entitled "The
Proverbs of Solomon" (Solomon 10:1–22:16). In
this section there are exactly 375 proverbs. Not
coincidentally, 375 is the numerical value of
Solomon's name.

Who Is Lady Wisdom?

In Proverbs 8, wisdom is personified as a woman.
It tells of her attributes and her creation by God.

She says "By me kings reign, and rulers decree what is just…. I love those who love me, and those who seek me diligently find me…. The Lord created me at the beginning of his work, the first of his acts of old."

The Lady and the Harlot

The author of Proverbs uses a vivid contrast to make a point about right living. He urges his son in chapter 7 to reject the "loose woman," the "harlot, wily of heart," warning him in detail of the dangers of the seductive call of the harlot who looks out of her window. Instead, the young man is urged to let himself be seduced by "Lady Wisdom" (chapter 8): "Does not wisdom call, does not understanding raise her voice?"

Wherever in the World Is Lady Wisdom?

Any computer game searching for Lady Wisdom would have to look at the 24th chapter of the apocryphal Book of Sirach. Here too wisdom is a woman, and she states that the Creator assigned her to "make your dwelling in…Israel…. I took root in an honored people" (Sirach 24:8,12). The key to wisdom, according to this chapter, is "the book of the covenant of the Most High God, the law that Moses commanded us."

Ecclesiastes: The Worldly Wise Preacher

The Book of Ecclesiastes is written by someone who has tried everything in search for meaning in life, but who has come up empty. It is full of frustration, even cynicism, but the book ends by affirming that life has meaning when lived in right relation with God. It is the closest piece of writing in the Bible to what the Greeks called philosophy.

Phantom Books

The Bible often refers to books that no longer exist. In the Old Testament, these include the Book of Jashar, the Book of the Wars of the Lord, the Chronicles of King David, and the Commentary of Iddo the Seer. In the New Testament, the Book of Enoch is mentioned, and several passages quote from other documents without naming them.

Song of Solomon: Love Songs

This book, also called the Song of Songs, is a beautiful collection of love poetry, much of which is rather explicit, even erotic. Some Jews and Christians have seen in the book a description of God's relationship with Israel or the Christian Church, and thereby avoided some of their embarrassment about the language of love.

Where Is God?

Two books in the Bible do not mention God even once: the Song of Solomon, which is a collection of love poetry, and the Book of Esther, which tells of the Jewish people's life and successes under Persian rule.

Isaiah: Prophet Par Excellence

The Book of Isaiah is arguably the greatest of the prophetic books. Its scope is all-encompassing. The book ranges from dramatic excoriations of wicked Judah to tender assurances of God's love and restoration to visions of the new heavens and the new earth. Many passages from Handel's *Messiah* are taken from Isaiah.

A Children's Ditty

The drunken prophets mocked Isaiah, comparing his words to a meaningless children's ditty:
"Do and do, do and do, rule on rule, rule on rule, a little here, a little there" (Isaiah 28:10).

Songs

Drinking songs are part of almost every culture, and the prophets Amos and Isaiah disapprovingly referred to them in biblical society. Isaiah even quotes two such songs: "Let us eat and drink, for tomorrow we die" (Isaiah 22:13). "'Come,' they say, 'let us get wine, let us fill ourselves with strong drink. And tomorrow will be like today, great beyond measure'" (Isaiah 56:12).

Playing With Words

Hebrew writers often used words that sounded similar to illustrate their ideas. The prophet Isaiah made an effective point about conditions in the land with the following word play:
"And God looked for justice (*mishpat*),
but he only found bloodshed (*mishpach*);
he looked for righteousness (*tsedaqah*),
but he only found a cry of distress (*tse`aqah*)!"
(Isaiah 5:7).

"The Sixth Sick Sheik's Sixth Sheep's Sick"

The Hebrew language may not have any tongue-twisters quite this difficult, but the use of assonance (successive words containing the same sounds) is common. One psalmist soothingly says, "*sha'alu shelom yerushalayim*" ("Pray for the peace of Jerusalem," Psalm 122:6). Isaiah packs a powerful punch by preaching that "*pachad wapachat wapach*" ("terror and pit and snare") will come upon the wicked (Isaiah 24:17).

What Was That Reference Again?

The New Testament often quotes from the Old Testament. However, sometimes it is not clear which passage is in view, as when Matthew quoted "He [Jesus] shall be called a Nazarene" (Matthew 2:23). Jesus was from Nazareth, but no such prophecy is found in the Old Testament. It may be a wordplay from Isaiah 11:1, which is a Messianic prophecy referring to the "branch" (Hebrew *nezer*).

Jeremiah and Lamentations: Books of Passion

The prophet Jeremiah revealed his personal passions more than any other prophet. He wept bitterly over the sins of his people, and argued bitterly with God for sending him as a prophet. He was vigorously opposed by false priests and prophets, and suffered much for his stand. The Book of Lamentations contains five passionate laments over the destruction of Jerusalem, traditionally ascribed to Jeremiah.

A Hebrew Cryptogram

A fascinating literary device found occasionally in the Hebrew Bible is called *atbash*. It created code words by substituting the first letter of the alphabet

The people mourn the ruins of Jerusalem.

for the last, the second for the next-to-last, and so on. A famous example is in Jeremiah 51:41, where Sheshach is a cryptogram for Babylon.

Lamentations and Acrostics

Perhaps the most emotional book in the Bible is the Book of Lamentations, which has five chapters of anguished laments over the destruction of Jerusalem. Strangely, these heart-felt laments are expressed in the rigid structure of the acrostic: each chapter has 22 verses (or a multiple of 22).

Ezekiel: Prophet in Exile

Ezekiel's book contains many strange visions and
strange actions. His message was to the Jews in
Babylonian exile, helping them to make sense of
their punishment and pointing them to a way of
restoration. Along with Jeremiah, he emphasized
the concept of each individual's responsibility for
his or her own sin, a concept that had been
forgotten in Judah. His book ends with a great
vision of the ideal temple.

Apocalyptic Literature

This is a type of Jewish and early Christian
literature that mostly dates from 200 B.C. to A.D.
100. It is rich with symbolism, angels, and other
spiritual beings; it communicates through dreams
and visions; and it is often very difficult to interpret
precisely. A major topic it addresses is the end of
time. In the Bible, the major apocalyptic portions
are Ezekiel 40 through 48, Daniel 7 through 12,
Zechariah 9 through 14, and the Book of
Revelation.

Faces and Wheels

Ezekiel had a glittering vision about four shining
manlike creatures that were accompanied by four
wheels (Ezekiel 1). The amazing creatures each
had four wings and four faces. The faces were
those of a man, a lion, an ox, and an eagle. The
wheels did not turn, but they had eyes in them,
and they flew wherever the creatures flew. The
symbolic vision portrayed God's majesty in vivid
and very poetic terms.

A Censored Chapter

The first chapter of the Book of Ezekiel may have portrayed God's majesty, but it was very strange. In fact, it was so difficult and so strange that Jewish young people under 30 years old were not allowed to read it!

Daniel's friends in the fiery furnace.

Daniel: Visionary Prophet

The Book of Daniel contains an equal mixture of stories about Daniel and his friends in exile—such as Daniel in the lions' den or his three friends

(Shadrach, Meshach, and Abednego) in the fiery furnace—and of visions about the future. The common thread between both parts of the book is the idea of God's control of the world's empires and his vindication of his people.

Can You Keep a Secret?

The Book of Daniel contains explicit words about the book's focus: Much of it was not for the present, but for a future time. Daniel was instructed in a vision to "seal up the vision, for it pertains to many days hence" (Daniel 8:26) and to "shut up the words, and seal the book, until the time of the end" (Daniel 12:4).

The Handwriting on the Wall

This common expression traces its origin to the Book of Daniel, when the Babylonian king Belshazzar was giving a great feast. We are told that a great hand appeared and began writing on the wall. The message was one of doom for this king, who was persecuting the Jews, and he died that very night.

An Aramaic Puzzle

The prophet Daniel was able to interpret the handwriting on the wall of King Belshazzar's palace. The words were *mene, mene, tekel, parsin,* which mean "numbered, weighed, divided." This signified that Belshazzar's days were numbered, that he had been weighed in the balance and found wanting, and that his kingdom would be divided among the Persians (whose name is a word play on *parsin*).

Hosea: Israel's Adultery

God told Hosea to marry a prostitute, and so he had to suffer her unfaithfulness. All of this was a metaphor for Israel's adultery against God when Israel followed other gods. The book speaks eloquently about Israel worshiping other gods and its neglect of social concerns.

Joel: The Day of the Lord

This short book focuses on the concept of the "Day of the Lord." This sometimes refers to God's immediate judgment on nations that oppressed others (such as in a great locust plague), and sometimes refers to God's judgment of all nations at the end of time. The Apostle Peter quoted extensively from Joel 2 (see Acts 2), applying its prophecies to his own day.

Amos: Israel's Social Conscience

Amos spoke out against social evils, such as abuse of power, oppression of the poor, dishonest dealings, and insincere religious ritual. He even spoke out against the life of leisure and the many possessions of the wealthy. These luxuries blinded the people to the very real needs around them.

A Pun-ishing Experience

Speakers of Hebrew loved a good pun. The prophet Amos was once shown a vision of a basket of "(ripe) summer fruit" (Hebrew *qayits*), to illustrate the point that the "end" (Hebrew *qets*) had come for Israel—the time was "ripe" for destruction (Amos 8:2).

Amos

Word-Links in the Bible

Sometimes word-links between adjacent books of
the Bible can be seen, which probably accounts for
their being placed together. The following phrase
occurs near the end of the Book of Joel (Joel 3:16):
"The Lord roars from Zion, and sends forth his
voice from Jerusalem." The next book, Amos,
begins with exactly the same phrase (Amos 1:2).

Obadiah: Edom's Doom

This shortest book in the Old Testament is a brief but concentrated blast of condemnation at Judah's neighbor Edom, located southeast of the Dead Sea. Edom had rejoiced at Jerusalem's downfall, and this book speaks about that.

Jonah: Prophet to Assyria

The message of this little jewel is often obscured by discussions about the fish that swallowed Jonah. It is a wonderful book about God's concern for all people, not just his chosen people. Jonah was sent to Nineveh, the capital of the world's largest empire, to urge its people to repent, and they did.

Micah: Typical Prophet

Micah fits well the stereotype of a biblical prophet, speaking out against both social and spiritual evils, and also looking into the future and speaking of the restoration of God's people. He predicted that the Messiah would come from Bethlehem, and he summarized well the duties of God's people: "And what does the Lord require of you but to do justice, and to love kindness, and to walk humbly with your God?" (Micah 6:8).

Chronology and the Order of the Bible's Books

In the Old Testament, the first 17 books (Genesis through Esther) are in essentially chronological order, beginning with creation and ending with the Jews in exile at the end of the Old Testament period. Other books are not grouped chronologically. The prophetic books are arranged with the three longest books first. Most of the prophets fit chronologically into the time period covered by the books of 1 and 2 Kings.

The Arrangement of the Prophetic Books

The longest prophetic books come first (Isaiah, Jeremiah, Ezekiel), the major prophets, and the 12 minor prophets follow. A rough (but not exact) chronological order can be seen here, since Hosea and Amos were the earliest prophets and they appear first, and Haggai, Zechariah, and Malachi, the later prophets, appear last.

Nahum and Zephaniah: Angry Prophets

These two minor prophets had short, intense messages. Nahum's was a quick, sustained blast of fury against Nineveh, the capital of the oppressive Assyrian Empire. Zephaniah's was a blast of judgment on Judah, Jerusalem, and Judah's enemies. The blasts of judgement were followed by God's promises of salvation.

Habakkuk: Questioning God

This wonderful little book, hidden away among the other minor prophets, questions why God would allow evil to run rampant in the world. It is a book that is similar to Job (both are known as theodicies—books that question God's justice). God's answer is that his justice will always prevail, even if it takes time. The Book of Habakkuk ends with a psalm that speaks joyfully of an encounter with God.

Haggai and Zechariah: Prophets of the Temple

Haggai and Zechariah both had messages for the community that had returned to Jerusalem after exile in Babylon. Haggai wrote about the rebuilding of the Temple, and Zechariah about the Temple and the future. Zechariah predicted the coming of Jerusalem's future king riding on a donkey, which Jesus did when he rode into Jerusalem the week before his death (celebrated by Christians as Palm Sunday).

Malachi: The Last Prophet

Malachi spoke about the abysmal conditions that existed after the Jews had settled and become complacent in their land once again. This included the corruption and neglect of the priesthood and the neglect of giving to God. His book ends with a prediction of the prophet Elijah's return, which the Book of Matthew applies to John the Baptist.

The "Hidden Books" Called the Apocrypha

The word *apocrypha* means "hidden," and it usually refers to 12 or more books added to the 39 books of the Hebrew Bible. These were written between 200 B.C. and A.D. 100, and are considered by many Christians to be part of the Bible since most were found in the first Greek translations of the Hebrew Bible. The Roman Catholic Church accepts 12 additional books, while Eastern Orthodox Churches accept 4 to 5 books beyond that.

Tobit and Judith:
Two Literary Masterpieces

Tobit and Sarah are the two righteous heroes of the Book of Tobit, both of whom are helped by the angel Raphael. Tobit was healed of blindness and Sarah was rid of a demon. Tobit is one of the most popular books of the Apocrypha. Judith is also a literary masterpiece. It tells of the Assyrian general Holofernes' war against the Jews and of the beautiful widow Judith's deadly trickery.

The Additions to Esther: Restoring God

The Greek translation of the Book of Esther has six substantial additions, which add 107 verses to the 167 verses of the Hebrew text. Their purpose is to give a clearly religious slant to the book. The extra verses make frequent reference to God, they emphasize his choice of Abraham and Israel, and they talk about prayer.

Wisdom of Solomon
and Sirach: Books of the Sages

These two apocryphal books are "wisdom" books in the tradition of the Book of Proverbs. Their subject matter ranges from practical advice in everyday living to mature philosophical reflections on the nature of wisdom itself. The Wisdom of Sirach is also known as Ecclesiasticus.

Baruch and the Letter of
Jeremiah: Help for Hard Times

Baruch was Jeremiah's secretary, and this book is supposed to be from him. It consists of confessions

Jeremiah dictates his book to Baruch.

of Israel's guilt after the fall of Jerusalem and two poems on wisdom and comfort in hard times. The Letter of Jeremiah is presented as Jeremiah's words to his followers. The letter expands on the thought in Jeremiah 10:11, which speaks of the reality of God and the unreality of idols.

The Additions to Daniel:
Entertaining Stories

Three apocryphal books contain additional stories about the prophet Daniel. The Song of the Three Jews contains prayers and hymns of Daniel's three friends (Shadrach, Meshach, and Abednego) who were thrown into the fiery furnace. The Book of Susanna tells of Daniel's rescue of Susanna, a woman who had been wronged. Bel and the Dragon tells two highly entertaining satirical tales that ridicule idolatry.

1 and 2 Maccabees:
Intertestamental History

These two lengthy books focus on the fortunes of the Jews from about 175 to 132 B.C. They tell of the Jews' revolt against intolerant Syrian rule, the Syrians' desecration of the Temple, the Jews' recapture of Jerusalem, and the Temple under Judas Maccabeus. They end with the establishment of Judea as an independent state.

The Book of Jashar

The Bible twice quotes from a book it calls the Book of Jashar (or the Book of the Upright One). The incident when God gave the Israelites victory over the Amorites when the sun and moon stood still in Joshua's day is said to have been recorded in this book (Joshua 10:13), as is David's lament over the deaths of Saul and Jonathan (2 Samuel 1:18). The book has not survived through the ages, however, although a late Jewish book of that title was written in an attempt to reproduce it.

Matthew: A Jewish Gospel

The Book of Matthew was written primarily for a Jewish audience. The book shows that Jesus was the Jewish Messiah, a king, and that he was descended from David and Abraham. Matthew records the story of the wise men visiting the baby Jesus, an event fitting for a king. Luke records the humbler story of the shepherds visiting Jesus.

Hunting for the Nativity

The most popular Christian holiday is Christmas, and yet the well-known and much-beloved Christmas stories of Jesus' birth are found in only two places in the Bible: Matthew 1 and 2, and Luke 1 and 2. Mark and John, both gospels about Jesus' life, don't even mention these wonderful stories.

The Nativity

Which Day Is Jesus' Birthday?

December 25 was celebrated as the birth date of
Jesus by the early fourth century A.D., and probably
much earlier. This date was probably selected
because the Romans celebrated the Mithraic festival
of the sun god on that day, and this was an
opportunity to make a pagan festival into a religious
one. This date was also near the winter solstice. The
Eastern Church celebrates Christmas on January 6.

Was Jesus Born "Before Christ"?

Jesus was born some time around the year 6 B.C.
King Herod, who attempted to kill baby Jesus by
killing all the Jewish male infants in and around
Bethlehem, died in 4 B.C. This discrepancy is owed
to the monk Dennis the Little, who in A.D. 532 came
up with the idea of marking years starting with
Christ's birth. Unfortunately, the year of Christ's
birth was not known until much more recently.

The Star in the East

The nature of the famous star that guided the wise
men has remained elusive. Scientific suggestions
have included a comet, a new star, a supernova, the
planet Venus, or a convergence of several planets. A
comet was recorded about 4 B.C., and Jupiter,
Mars, and Saturn converged in the constellation
Pisces in 6 B.C. Both of these events could fit the
biblical story.

Who Were the Magi?

The Greek historian Herodotus (fifth century B.C.)
spoke of magi who were a priestly tribe in the

The three magi search for the Christ child.

Persian empire. Later (in the Book of Acts), the term refers to anyone who practiced magic arts (the word "magic" comes from *magi*). The most famous magi were the wise men who visited the baby Jesus. Matthew states that they came to Bethlehem from the East; tradition has located this in Persia, Babylonia, or Arabia.

How Many Wise Men?

Tradition has it that three wise men came from the East to visit the baby Jesus. Traditionally, their names were Melchior, Gaspar, and Balthasar. In fact, the Gospel of Matthew mentions neither their names nor how many there were. The number three arose from the gifts of gold, frankincense, and myrrh that they brought.

Mark: An Action-Packed Gospel

Mark's account of Jesus' life is the shortest and the most action-oriented. Mark portrays Jesus as one who was constantly serving others. Mark records 18 miracles and only 4 full parables. In contrast, a much greater emphasis on Jesus' teachings is in the other gospels.

Luke: Beloved Physician's Gospel

Luke was the only Gentile among the New Testament's authors, and he wrote for a Gentile audience. As a medical doctor, he tells us that he investigated his subject matter thoroughly before setting forth his account (Luke 1:1–4), and his eye for details is evident. His book also has a warm, human touch to it.

Jesus' Blasphemy?

In the course of a debate with a group of Jews, Jesus claimed to have seen Abraham. When they challenged this statement, he replied, "before Abraham was, I am" (John 8:58). The Jews were enraged with this reference to "I am," since only God was to be referred to in this way. They considered this blasphemy, and tried to stone Jesus to death. This is one of the most direct statements in the Gospels equating Jesus with God.

The Parables of Jesus

Jesus' favorite teaching tool was the parable. In its simplest form, the parable uses a comparison to make a point. It is simple, direct, and the point is clear, such as "The kingdom of heaven is like treasure hidden in a field, which someone found and hid; then in his joy he goes and sells all that he has and buys that field" (Matthew 13:44).

Extended Parables

Many of Jesus' parables were stories. They involved comparisons, and the characters often represented God the Father or Jesus himself. Among the most beloved extended parables are the shepherd who risks all to search for his one lost sheep, the father who eagerly takes back his long-wayward son, and the good Samaritan who stopped to help a robbery victim when members of society's elite would not.

John: A Theological Gospel

The Apostle John's picture of Jesus is the most theological of the four Gospels. His focus is upon Jesus as the Son of God the Father. His book is addressed to the world at large, and his purpose was to convince people that Jesus was the Messiah, the Son of God (John 20:31). The action is slower than in Mark's Gospel, with more attention to conversations and teaching.

The Eye of a Needle

Jesus used hyperbole when he said, "It is easier for a camel to go through the eye of a needle than for a rich man to enter the kingdom of God"

(Mark 10:25). An unfounded tradition that this referred to a small pedestrian gate in the center of Jerusalem's huge wooden gates arose in the Middle Ages to soften the import of this proverb.

Jesus' Crucifixion

Jesus' crucifixion followed typical Roman procedures. He was publicly whipped, forced to carry his own cross, and nailed to it. A tablet identifying him was attached to the upright above his head. Contrary to custom, however, his legs were not broken to hasten his death, since he was already dead when the soldiers came to do it. The Gospel of John states (19:36) that this fulfilled an Old Testament prophecy.

Resurrection from the Dead in the Bible

The Bible tells of many people coming back to life after having been dead. In the Old Testament, a widow's son was brought back to life by Elijah (1 Kings 17); the son of a wealthy couple was raised by Elisha (2 Kings 4); and a man whose corpse was thrown into Elisha's grave came back to life (2 Kings 13). In the New Testament, a widow's son (Luke 7), Jairus's daughter (Luke 8), and Lazarus (John 11) were raised by Jesus. Dorcas (also known as Tabitha) was brought back to life by Peter (Acts 9). Paul brought back Eutychus (Acts 20). Many believers were raised at the time of Jesus' death (Matthew 27). The most significant resurrection, of course, was Jesus himself (Matthew 28). Jesus' resurrection presented his decisive triumph over the power of sin and death.

Christ's Crucifixion

The Acts of the Apostles:
After the Resurrection

The Book of Acts tells the story of the early
Christian church, written by Luke as a sequel to his

account of Jesus. Luke showed the movement of the newly proclaimed message of Jesus Christ from its Jerusalem-based beginnings rooted in Judaism to its becoming a world-wide, inclusive faith that reached all the way to Rome.

"Abba, Father"

The Aramaic word abba is an intimate form of the word *ab*, which means "father." It was an informal term of intimacy and respect used by children, something like da-da or daddy. Jesus used this term in Mark 14:36 to describe the intimate and loving relationship that believers could have with God the Father.

Epithets of God

The Bible has many epithets for God. These include Almighty, Anchor, Ancient of Days, Delight, Dwelling Place, Judge, King, Most High, Redeemer, Righteousness, Rock, Savior, Shepherd, Strength, and Vindicator. A set of famous epithets (titles) for the Messiah, found in a stirring passage from Handel's *Messiah*, are from Isaiah 9:5: "Wonderful Counselor, Mighty God, Everlasting Father, Prince of Peace."

Messiah: One Who Is Anointed

Our word Messiah comes from the Hebrew word *mashiach*, which means "anointed one." In the Old Testament, kings were anointed into their office; so any number of kings could be called messiahs. The New Testament presents Jesus as the Messiah, the one ultimate and perfect king.

Immanuel: God With Us

One of the most famous prophecies about the Messiah is found in Isaiah 7:14, where a virgin is to conceive and bear a son named Immanuel. This name is *Imma-nu-el* in Hebrew, literally translated it means "with us (is) God." Matthew 1:23 quotes this as having been fulfilled in Jesus.

The Annunciation

Jesus: One Who Saves

The name Jesus (in Greek *Iesous*) is related to the Hebrew names Joshua and Isaiah, which mean "one who saves" or "Yahweh saves." The angel told Jesus' mother, Mary, to call him Jesus, because he would save his people from their sins (Matthew 1:21).

Jesus, the Christ

Christ was not part of the name that Mary gave Jesus. The term is a title, and it comes from the Greek word for "messiah" (*christos*). Thus, Jesus was often referred to as "the Christ" (the Messiah). Jesus' friends would have called him Yeshua, the Aramaic word for Jesus.

Romans: Paul's System of Faith

The Book of Romans is a letter written to Christians in Rome to explain Paul's understanding of what the Christian faith was about. This book is the most systematic and theological of his letters. The first half emphasizes the theme of righteousness and how to attain it, and the last chapters are practical exhortations about living.

INRI: Jesus of Nazareth, King of the Jews

All four Gospels state that a plaque was placed on Jesus' cross identifying him. John states that it was written in Hebrew, Latin, and Greek. The letters "INRI," often seen on this plaque in paintings of Jesus' crucifixion, represent the Latin words for the phrase, "Jesus of Nazareth, King of the Jews."

A Secret Password

The fish was an early symbol of Christianity, since the Greek word for fish, *ichthus,* is an acronym (the first letter of each word) for the Greek phrase *Iesous Christos Theou Huios Soter,* which means "Jesus Christ, of God the Son, Savior." It was written as graffiti, and was used as a secret password when Christians were being persecuted by the Romans.

1 and 2 Corinthians: Problem Solving

The church at Corinth, Greece, had many problems. Paul's letters to them—there were at least four, but only two are preserved—address these problems one by one. These problems included factions in the church, incest, marriage, food offered to idols, spiritual gifts (such as speaking in unintelligible tongues), opposition to Paul, and the concept of resurrection.

Galatians: Freedom from Legalism

Since all the early Christians were Jews, a question arose about Christians keeping all the Jewish laws, including circumcision. This letter was Paul's statement that Christians were made right with God only by their faith.

An Early Christian Hymn

The Apostle Paul occasionally used the words of early Christian hymns when he wrote his letters. The most famous example of this is found in Philippians 2:5–11, where a soaring passage about Christ's humility, humiliation, and ultimate exaltation is found.

Psalms, Hymns, and Spiritual Songs

The Apostle Paul twice mentions the songs of Christian worship in his letters. He urges people to sing "psalms and hymns and spiritual songs" with great joy and thanksgiving (Ephesians 5:19; Colossians 3:16). These included the words of Scripture (psalms), as well as songs of praise (hymns) and other types of songs (spiritual songs).

Ephesians, Philippians, Colossians: Prison Letters

The Apostle Paul spent much time in prison for his faith, and there he wrote several letters to churches. In these letters, he encouraged three different churches to know clearly what they believe and to put these beliefs into practice.

1 and 2 Thessalonians: The End of Time

Paul gave the church at Thessalonica, Greece, encouragement and instruction in these two letters. This included much teaching about the return of Christ to earth at the end of time. This church must have had a special interest in the subject.

St. Paul preaches to the Thessalonians.

1 and 2 Timothy, Titus: Pastoral Letters

These letters were to two people who were ministers (or pastors) of churches. The letters gave specific instructions about the orderly functioning of churches, and for resisting false teachings.

Inter-Biblical Quotes

The New Testament quotes the Old Testament hundreds of times, but only once does a New Testament author mention another New Testament writer by name. Peter cites Paul in support of his own views on God's patience (2 Peter 3:15).

Philemon: On Slavery

This is one of Paul's most intensely personal letters. It is a friendly, tactful letter to his friend Philemon, who owned a runaway slave. This slave had been captured, and he converted to Christianity under Paul in prison. Paul asked Philemon to welcome the slave as a Christian brother.

Hebrews: Book of Better Things

The author of this book forcefully makes the point that Jesus was the perfect fulfillment of much prophecy in the Old Testament. The book stresses the importance of faith.

James: Faith in Action

Whereas Romans, Galatians, and Hebrews stress the importance of faith alone in one's relationship to God, the Book of James presents the case that faith without good works to demonstrate this faith is dead intellectualism.

Fanciful Interpretation

Allegorical interpretation was popular early in
church history. Here is part of one early church
father's (Origen's) interpretation of the parable of
the Good Samaritan:

The man going down to Jericho = Adam
Jerusalem, his starting-point = Paradise
Jericho = This world
Robbers = Hostile
influences and
enemies
Wounds = Sins
Priest = Law
Levites = Prophets
Good Samaritan = Christ
Beast = Body of Christ
Inn = Church
Innkeeper = Guardian angels
Return of good Samaritan = Second coming
of Christ

Hagar the Mountain

An allegory is a story that carries (or gives in its
interpretation) a hidden meaning, or, more
commonly, several hidden meanings. A well-known
example is from the Apostle Paul, when he speaks
of Abraham's two wives, Sarah and Hagar. He says
"Now this is an allegory: these women are two
covenants .... Now Hagar is Mount Sinai...."
(Galatians 4:24, 25). He also compares Hagar with
the earthly Jerusalem and Sarah with the heavenly
city.

An angel appears to Hagar in the desert.

Fables in the Bible

Fables are fictitious stories that make a concise moral point; they often employ animals or plants as speaking characters. A well-known fable in the Bible is the one told by Jotham about the trees. It begins "The trees once went forth to anoint a king over them; and they said to the olive tree, 'Reign over us.'"

Herod the Fox

Metaphors are figures of speech in which a term describing a certain object is used to describe something else for the purpose of making a vivid comparison. This was a rhetorical device that Jesus often used. He called King Herod "that fox"

(Luke 13:32). He called himself "the bread of life" (John 6:35) and "the true vine" (John 15:1). He even called some who came to follow him "you brood of vipers!" (Luke 3:7).

1 and 2 Peter: Crisis Management

The Apostle Peter's two letters offer encouragement to those suffering persecution. Peter reminds them of their fellow sufferer and the perfect example, Jesus. These letters also warn against false teachings.

1, 2, and 3 John: Truth and Love

John's letters deal with truth in the face of false teaching, especially early Gnosticism (intellectual knowledge can lead to salvation). In his first letter, he also emphasizes right relationship with God through Jesus Christ, and the importance of love in all areas of our life.

Jude: Eclectic Warnings

This short book warns against false teachings, much in the way that 2 Peter does. A distinctive aspect of Jude is that it quotes from nonbiblical books, such as the Assumption of Moses (in verse 9) and the Book of Enoch (in verse 14).

Revelation: Visions of the End

The Book of Revelation presents the Apostle John's visions of the end of time. The book is rich with symbols and strange creatures, such as angels, dragons, and beasts, great armies and cataclysmic battles, a lake of fire, and a bottomless pit. The consistent message of the book is the ultimate and

St. John writes his book.

final triumph of Christ over the devil and all forces
of evil.

Beasts and Dragons

The Book of Revelation is the longest example of
apocalyptic literature in the Bible. It speaks of great
hosts of angels, and a great red dragon with seven
heads and ten horns and seven crowns on its heads.
This book describes several beasts, one that looked
like a leopard with feet like a bear's and a mouth
like a lion's. The dragon and the beasts are symbols
of the devil.

A Bold Translator

Latin was the language of the Roman Empire, and
so, in about A.D. 382, Pope Damasus I commissioned Jerome to produce an authoritative
translation of the Bible. Jerome did, but he shocked
the world by translating directly from the Hebrew
text, rather than from the Greek Septuagint or
earlier Latin versions, as had been the practice. His
version was called the Vulgate.

**The Printing Press: A
Revolutionary Technology**

When the Bible was copied by hand, copies were
too expensive for common people. Also, copy
mistakes crept into the process. The invention of
the printing press revolutionized production of the
Bible and other books. Now hundreds—and even
thousands—of copies could be printed, each exactly
the same as the other. This made it possible for
almost anyone to have a Bible.

Gutenberg's Bible: The World's First Printed Book

A German named Johann Gutenberg produced the first printed Bible in 1456. It was written in Latin, the language of the Catholic Church. Gutenberg experimented for many years in developing his printing press before he perfected what people called artificial writing. There are fewer than 50 copies of the Gutenberg Bible in existence today.

Gutenberg's Printing Press

Each page of Gutenberg's Bible was produced by using hundreds of pieces of *movable type* made from molten lead, tin, and other metals. Each piece represented a letter. These made up the printing plates, which were held in a bed, and the ink was rolled over them. Then an impression of each page was literally pressed onto blank sheets of paper, which were held by a platen. The type used in Gutenberg's Bible looks very much like handwriting.

Bible Printing Today

Modern Bibles are printed using space-age technologies. The pages still must be pressed onto blank sheets of paper, but this is now done by lightning-fast methods. There are better ways of transferring the ink onto paper, better inks, and better paper. Also, the Bible is now on computer disk and on audiocassette tapes in many languages. Many Bibles are red-letter editions, where Jesus' words are printed in red ink.

The First English Bibles

The first complete English Bible was not the King James Bible. It was John Wycliffe's translation in the late 1300s, based on the Latin Vulgate. It was the main English version until William Tyndale's version appeared, about 1525. Tyndale translated the Old Testament directly from the Hebrew, the first version since Jerome's to do so.

William Tyndale's Bible: Inflammatory Version

When Tyndale was working on his English translation, Church officials were the Bible authorities. His translation threatened the Church's monopoly on Bible learning, so he had to have his English Bible printed in Germany. Because of this, Tyndale was arrested and burned to death at the stake. Thousands of copies of his Bible were seized and publicly burned.

The Geneva Bible

An English Bible was produced in 1560 at Geneva, Switzerland, the city of John Calvin. It was the first to print each verse as a separate paragraph, and it introduced the convention (which remains even today in the King James Bible) of italicizing words that were not in the original languages but were added by the translators in order to make sense of a passage.

The World's Oldest Bible Publisher

The longest-running publisher of Bibles is the Cambridge University Press. The Press began

The right of the University of Cambridge to print and sell all manner of books was granted by Henry VIII in 1534. The University has printed and published continuously since 1584.

printing Bibles in 1591 with the Geneva Version of the Bible, and it has continued ever since. Today it still has a reputation of producing fine-quality Bibles.

The King James Bible

King James I of England commissioned a unique Bible, without doctrinal marginal notes (which were common in other Bibles of the time). It was written in the common English language of the day, and it appeared in 1611. This Bible achieved a remarkable success, maintaining its place as the preeminent English Bible for well over 300 years.

The Wicked Bible

Some humorous typographical errors were made in early editions of the King James Bible. Probably the most famous was the omission of the word "not" in the seventh commandment, and thus it read "Thou shalt commit adultery." This edition was dubbed the Wicked Bible. For this error, the King's printers were fined 300 pounds by the archbishop!

So Many Bible Versions!

Major revisions of the King James Bible began in 1885, and have continued to the present. There has been a virtual explosion of Bible translations in the past three decades. The English-speaking public has more than 70 versions of the Bible (or parts of it) to choose from!

Literal Bible Versions

Many English Bible versions aim at word-for-word accuracy—at literal translation. That is the principle that has guided such versions as the King James Bible and its revisions, which include the New American Standard Version, the Revised Standard Version, and the New King James Version. These Bibles are useful for careful study.

Dynamic Bible Versions

Most modern English Bible versions aim at "dynamic equivalency"—which means they are translated phrase-by-phrase, or thought-by-thought. These versions aren't translated strictly word-for-word. These are smoother translations and are good for reading large portions of Scripture. These include the New International Version, the Revised English and American Bibles, and the Jewish Publication Society's Tanakh.

Paraphrase Versions

Some English versions are not, strictly speaking, translations, but rather paraphrases. Translators have rewritten and paraphrased entire sentences or verses, often making two or three sentences out of a short phrase or sentence in other versions. The Living Bible and Today's English Version (*Good News for Modern Man*) are the most famous paraphrases. These are especially helpful for first-time Bible readers.

Abridged Bibles

A number of condensed Bibles have appeared in the twentieth century, where repetitive portions were deleted and other portions were briefly summarized. The Reader's Digest Bible is a true abridgement. It retains the text of the Revised Standard Version, but repetitive sections, unnecessary words, and portions thought to be less important than others have been deleted. It is a good Bible for people who have never read the Bible before.

Children's Bibles

Many Bibles written especially for children also exist. Some are mostly pictures and simple retellings of Bible stories. These are simple enough for two- to three-years-olds to understand. Others are written for grade-school children who have beginning reading vocabularies. Many have questions after each story. Other editions are written for teenagers. There are even comic book editions of the Bible!

A Down-Home Bible

Clarence Jordan's Cottonpatch Version of the Bible used contemporary Southern people, places, and parties in place of the biblical ones. Corinth became Atlanta, Jews became whites and Gentiles became Negroes, and the city of Rome became Washington, D.C.

A Seaman's Bible

Paraphrasing with a vengeance was Captain J. Rogers's practice in his Seaman's Version of the Bible. In Psalm 23, for example, instead of the familiar "The Lord is my shepherd, I shall not want," Rogers had "The Lord is my Pilot; I shall not drift."

Best-Selling Book

The Bible is consistently the world's best-selling book. Between 1815 and 1975, an estimated 2.5 billion Bibles were printed. The best-selling versions are the King James Version, the New International Version, and the Living Bible, which sell millions each year. In addition, millions of copies of the Bible and portions of it, such as the New Testament and Psalms, are given away free each year.

Bible Translations

Portions of the Bible have been translated into about 2,000 of the more than 6,000 known languages today, including close to 400 complete Bible translations. Most of the world's languages are minor languages of small, remote tribes or groups. Many organizations work at translating the Bible into most of the remaining languages. The goal is not 100 percent translation though, since many people can speak or read more than their own native language.

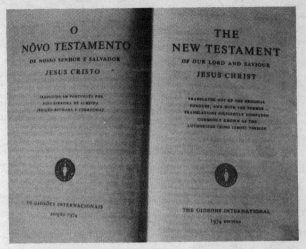

The New Testament in Spanish and English

The Most Expensive Bible

The world's most expensive Bible is the copy of Gutenberg's Old Testament, containing Genesis through Psalms. It was printed in 1455, and it brought $5.39 million at an auction at Christie's in New York on October 22, 1987.

The Earliest Biblical Texts

The earliest biblical texts in existence today are two short fragments found inscribed on two beautiful silver amulets. These were discovered in 1979 alongside the Scottish Church in Jerusalem. They date to about the time of the destruction of Jerusalem in 587 B.C., and they contain the words of Numbers 6:22–27. This is the priestly benediction known as the Aaronic Blessing.

The Oldest Hebrew Bible

The oldest complete version of the Hebrew Bible still in existence dates from A.D. 1008. It is part of a valuable and comprehensive collection of old Hebrew manuscripts in the Russian Public Library in St. Petersburg (formerly Leningrad), brought there in the late 1800s. It is known as the Leningrad Codex.

The Oldest Greek New Testament

The oldest complete version of the New Testament (as well as the Greek Old Testament) is a book written on parchment dating to the fourth century A.D. It is called the Codex Sinaiticus, because it was discovered in a monastery on Mount Sinai in the middle of the 1800s. It was purchased from the Soviet government in 1933 by the British government for 100,000 pounds, and it is now in the British Museum in London.

Where's That Reference Again?

The Bible was not written with chapter or verse numbers, which made it difficult to locate specific texts. The first paragraph markings of the Hebrew Bible were before the Christian Era, and division by verse was introduced by Jewish scribes soon after the time of Christ. Chapter divisions of both Old and New Testaments came in the thirteenth century.

Can't They Count?!

In many places, the verse numbering in the English Old Testament differs slightly from that in the

Hebrew Bible, even though the contents are exactly the same. Most often this happens in Psalms, where English Bibles do not number the titles of the ancient psalms, while the Hebrew Bible does.

The Samaritan Pentateuch

An early Hebrew version was the popularizing revision of the Bible's first five books (the Pentateuch) made in the Samaritan community north of Jerusalem, which arose some time after 722 B.C. It differs in some 6,000 places with the major Hebrew manuscripts available today. Many are trivial differences, but some reflect the Samaritans' emphasis on certain of their own doctrines.

Samaritan Distinctives

The Samaritans were Israelites who arose in and around Samaria and Mount Gerizim after the Assyrians sacked the city in 722 B.C. They were conservative in doctrine: They only accepted the Pentateuch as Scripture. Occasionally they made changes for doctrinal reasons, such as the substitution of Mount Gerizim (which was their sacred mountain) for Mount Ebal in Deuteronomy 27:4, as the place where the law was to be written on the altar.

What Is the Tanakh?

This is what Jews call their Bible, and it is the acronym for the Hebrew Bible. The word is based upon the three divisions of the Hebrew Bible: the Law, the Prophets, and the Writings. The Hebrew words for these are *Torah, Nebi'im, and Kethubim*. The first letters of these three words are T-N-K, which come together in the word Tanakh.

The Talmud: Jewish Teaching

The Hebrew word *talmud* means both" learning" and "teaching." As a title, it refers to two great collections of Jewish learning, which are based upon the Bible. These are the exhaustive Babylonian Talmud, collected in the fifth century A.D. and the shorter Jerusalem Talmud, collected somewhat earlier. The Pharisees were the guardians of the Jewish traditions that made their way into the Talmud.

The Mishnah: Collection of Jewish Law and Ethics

The Mishnah ("teaching by repetition") is the first part (and core) of the Talmud and ranks second only to the Bible itself. It is divided into six parts. The first is Seeds, which are eleven tractates dealing with agricultural regulations. The second is Festivals, which are twelve tractates dealing with the festivals. The third is Women, which are seven tractates (treatises) on marriage and divorce. The fourth is Damages—these are ten tractates on civil and criminal laws. The fifth is Sacred Things, which are eleven tractates on sacrifices. The last and sixth is Cleanness—these twelve tractates are on ritual cleanness and uncleanness.

The Gemara: Amplification of the Mishnah

The Gemara ("learning") is the second part of the Talmud, and it amplifies and comments upon the

Mishnah, the Talmud's first part. It was written in Aramaic (the Mishnah was written in Hebrew). Together, the Mishnah and the Gemara comprise the full Talmud. The Babylonian Talmud is 5,894 folio pages in length, and is 12 large volumes.

"The Ocean of the Talmud"

The subject matter of the Babylonian Talmud (which has been the standard Talmud for most Jews) is so extensive that the phrase "the ocean of the Talmud" arose to describe it. A prominent editor of the *Encyclopedia of Jewish Concepts* comments that it includes "religion and ethics, exegesis and homiletics, jurisprudence and ceremonial laws, ritual and liturgy, philosophy and science, medicine and magic, astronomy and astrology, history and geography, commerce and trade, politics and social problems."

A Rabbi's Good Advice

Constant study of the Law was very important in the Jewish community. Psalm 1:2 states that the righteous person's delight is in meditating day and night on the Law. The great rabbi Hillel encouraged frequent repetition in such study by saying that "reviewing a lesson a hundred times cannot be compared with reviewing it a hundred and one times."

The Wisdom of the Talmud

Many sayings in the Talmud are reminiscent of those in the Book of Proverbs. Here are some samples: "I have learned much from my teachers, even more from my colleagues, but I have learned the most from my students." "He who seeks a friend without faults will remain friendless." "No one should taunt a reformed sinner about his past."

A Man and His Wife in the Talmud

The Talmud contains many wise sayings about marriage: "Love your wife as much as yourself, but honor her more than yourself." "If your wife is short, bend your head and take her advice." "A man should eat and drink beneath his means, clothe himself within his means, and honor his wife above his means."

Midrash: Jewish Commentary

The term *midrash* means "investigation" or "commentary." Many books called midrashes arose between A.D. 200 and 1000, commenting on books of the Hebrew Bible from legal, ethical, or devotional perspectives. The midrashes contain many stories with morals to them (like Aesop's fables) and many ethical maxims.

The Masoretes: Jewish Guardians of the Scriptures

Hebrew was originally written without vowels, spaces between words, or punctuation. The Masoretes were Jewish scribes who first appeared in the second century A.D. and who flourished in the sixth through tenth centuries A.D. They devised a system of word, phrase, sentence, and paragraph divisions, as well as a detailed system for representing the vowels and accents on words. This insured that the Hebrew Scriptures would be uniformly copied, pronounced, and interpreted.

The Masorah: A Fence for the Law

The system of vowel and accent markings, as well as the Masoretes' many marginal notations about individual words and phrases, was called the Masorah. It protected the biblical text from misunderstanding and misinterpretation. A famous rabbinic quote about the Masorah is that it serves as "a fence for the Torah," i.e., to protect it.

The Torah: The Ladder of Sinai

Jacob dreamed about a ladder he saw ascending into heaven. The numerical value of the Hebrew word for ladder equals that of the word Sinai. Thus, the rabbis argued that the Torah—the Law of Moses—which was revealed at Mount Sinai, was the ladder that leads from earth to heaven.

The Longest Book in the Bible

The Book of Jeremiah is the longest book in the Bible. It has the most words, even though it doesn't have the most chapters (52). Jeremiah was a passionate prophet, pouring out his heart at great length and with great emotion to God. The book with the most chapters is the Book of Psalms, with 150 separate psalms.

The Longest Chapter in the Bible

The longest chapter in the Bible is Psalm 119, with 176 verses. It is an acrostic poem, with each group of eight verses beginning with successive letters of the alphabet. This psalm is a massive composition in praise of the Torah (the Law). Each verse refers to God's Word in some way.

The Longest Verse in the Bible

The Book of Esther contains the longest verse in the Bible: Esther 8:9. It consists of 85 words in the New Revised Standard Version, 43 words in the Hebrew. Its subject matter is rather mundane: It tells of Mordechai (Esther's adoptive father) issuing an edict.

The Shortest Book in the Bible

The Book of 3 John is the shortest book in the Bible, with 19 less words than its companion book, 2 John. Both of these were about one papyrus sheet in length. Five books share the distinction of being only one chapter long: Obadiah (in the Old Testament) and Philemon, 2 John, 3 John, and Jude (in the New Testament).

The Shortest Chapter in the Bible

The Bible's shortest chapter comes just two chapters before its longest chapter: Psalm 117. It is a beautiful little gem, a burst of praise to God, urging people to praise God for his goodness and faithfulness. It is only two verses long!

The Shortest Verse in the Bible

The Bible's shortest verse is John 11:35, "Jesus wept." This happened when Jesus heard that his friend Lazarus had died, so he performed a miracle and brought Lazarus back from the dead.

Methuselah: Just One of the Boys

Many people know that Methuselah was the oldest man in the Bible, living 969 years. However, he was not unique for his time. Jared lived for 962 years, Noah lived for 950 years, Seth lived for 912 years, Enosh lived for 905 years, and Mahalalel lived for 895 years. The first man, Adam, lived for 930 years.

The Most Wives

Solomon had the most recorded wives in the Bible: 300 wives who were princesses and 700 concubines (female slaves). Many of his marriages were political. They were tokens of an alliance with foreign kings with whom Solomon had accepted daughters in exchange for promises of peace.

The Most Husbands

The Sadducees told Jesus of a woman who had had seven husbands, all brothers (Matthew 22). Each one had died, and the next had married the woman.

Jesus himself encountered a woman who had had five husbands, and who was currently living with a man who was not her husband (John 4).

The Tallest Man in the Bible

Goliath was the Bible's tallest man. He was a Philistine giant who measured "six cubits and a span," or about 9½ feet tall. King Saul was also tall. His height is given as being "head and shoulders above everyone else."

The Shortest Man in the Bible

No short person's height is actually given, but Zacchaeus was noted for his short stature. Luke 19 tells us that when Jesus came to town, Zacchaeus climbed a tree to see him because he (Zacchaeus) was too short to see over the crowd. Some people joke that Job's friend Bildad the Shuhite ("shoe-height") was the world's shortest man.

Twenty-Four Fingers and Toes!

A Philistine giant mentioned in 1 Chronicles 20:6 had six fingers on each hand and six toes on each foot. This phenomenon (called polydactylism) is commonly known from ancient texts and art. In an early temple in Jericho, a six-toed clay statue was found. In Assyria, a child with six fingers on the left hand was considered a good sign, but six fingers on the right hand was a sign of bad fortune.

The Smallest Seed

The smallest seed mentioned in the Bible is the tiny mustard seed. The mustard plant grew into

David defeats Goliath.

something close to five feet tall, however. Jesus used it to characterize the growth of God's kingdom, from something small (the tiny seed) to something great (the large plant), as well as to speak of the tiny amount of faith needed to work wonders.

The Most Generous Person in the Bible

This honor belongs to the poor widow Jesus saw dropping two small copper coins into the treasury boxes in the Temple. These were the smallest coins in circulation, worth less than a penny, and yet they were the last things she owned. Thus, she gave "all she had to live on" (Mark 12:44).

An Alphabet Story

Arabbinic story tells how each letter asked God to create the world using a word that began with it. However, beginning from the end of the alphabet, each letter was disqualified, because an unfavorable word also began with it. This lasted until the second letter (beth), which was given the honor: The word *bara* ("to create") begins with beth. The first letter of the alphabet (aleph) had the honor of beginning the Ten Commandments.

"Moses Breaketh the Tablets" by Edward Lanning

A Is for Ox

The earliest alphabets used pictures of common objects to represent the sounds of the first letters of these words. The first letter of the Hebrew alphabet is the *aleph,* derived from *alpu* "ox," and so the first *aleph* was a line drawing of an ox head. Through a series of linguistic steps, it is the ancestor of the English capital *A.*

Let's Learn the *Aleph-Beth!*

The English word alphabet traces its origins to Hebrew. It comes from the first two Greek letters, *alpha* and *beta.* But the Greeks borrowed their alphabet from the Phoenicians (close cousins to the Hebrews), whose alphabet began with *aleph* and *beth,* the Phoenician-Hebrew words for "ox" and "house."

Jots and Tittles

When Jesus said, "one jot or one tittle shall in no way pass from the law, till all be fulfilled" (Matthew 5:18), he affirmed the importance of the Old Testament law. The "jot" was the *yodh,* the smallest letter of the Hebrew alphabet, while the "tittle" was only part of a letter: a small pen stroke.

Blessings From A to Z

In Jewish tradition, God blesses Israel from "aleph to taw." These Hebrew letters are the first and last in the Hebrew alphabet, so the expression means God blesses Israel completely. By striking coincidence, the list of blessings found in Leviticus 26:3–13 begins with aleph and ends with taw!

Lip-Reading

St. Augustine once saw St. Ambrose reading the
Bible silently. This surprised him so much that he
commented on the fact that Ambrose was reading
"without moving his lips." In the ancient world,
reading—even to oneself—was always done aloud.

The Alpha and Omega

Alpha and omega are the first and last letters of
the Greek alphabet. The expression "the Alpha and
Omega" is used three times in the book of
Revelation, referring to God the Father (twice)
and the Son (once). The phrase "I am the Alpha
and the Omega" means "I am the beginning and
the end."

Strange Meditations

The Hebrew word for "meditation" (*hagah*) is also
used to describe the coo of a dove, the growl of a
lion, the plotting of evil rulers, as well as the
reading of the Bible. These things are all something
done audibly. Thus, when Jews were instructed to
"meditate" on God's word (Psalm 1:2), this meant
that they should recite it aloud to themselves.

Ancient Scribes

The scribes were the ancient world's educated elite.
They were the guardians of the very complex
writing traditions, which required years of study to
master. Scribes learned in scribal schools, where
they copied ancient texts by the dozen. They
served kings in all societies, including Israel and
Judah.

Jesus preaches in the synagogue.

Scribes as Religious Authorities

After Jerusalem and the Temple were destroyed by
the Babylonians in 586 B.C., the study of the Mosaic
Law (the Torah) grew in importance, and the
scribes became a professional class of Torah scholars.
In the New Testament, Jesus had many disputes
over interpretation of the Law with the scribes and
Pharisees.

Ashurbanipal's Library

The Assyrian king Ashurbanipal was by far the
greatest patron of literature in the pre–Christian Era.
He amassed a royal library of more than 26,000
historical, religious, and scientific texts at his capital
of Nineveh. He commissioned his emissaries to
search the world and bring back copies of every
known text. The discovery of this library in 1853
revealed a large portion of what we know today of
ancient Mesopotamia.

Ancient Law Codes

The Mosaic Law contains 613 specific commandments regulating most aspects of people's lives and worship, but this is not the earliest example of an ancient law code. The Sumerians developed the first such codes in the early second millennium B.C. The most systematic law code was the Babylonian king Hammurabi's (about 1792 to 1750 B.C.), and the Hittites also developed an extensive law code in the thirteenth century B.C.

mrhdlttllmb

This is "Mary had a little lamb," written without any vowels, word divisions, or punctuation. The Old Testament was originally written without any of these, and readers had to supply these themselves in order to make sense of the text.

Scapegoat or Demon?

The word "scapegoat" comes from the King James Version of the Bible. In Leviticus 16 a goat was banished to the wilderness after Israel's sins were symbolically transferred onto its head (the "escape goat"). However, the Hebrew term in question, *azazel,* was probably the name of a desert demon, and the goat was sent "to Azazel" (to remove Israel's sin completely).

Did Adam Speak Hebrew?

The words of Adam recorded in the Scriptures are in Hebrew, but he probably did not speak this language. Hebrew was not identifiable as a language until the second half of the second millennium B.C.

Therefore, we do not know the precise language of early Bible people such as Adam, Noah, or Abraham.

Coming or Going?

An early way of writing among the Greeks—soon abandoned—was done in a forward-backward mode, like a field is plowed. The Greek term for this was *boustrophedon* (which means "as the ox turns"). Here is a familiar nursery rhyme written this way:

Humpty Dumpty sat on a wall
ytpmuD ytpmuH
had a great fall.
sesroh s'gnik eht llA
and all the king's men
ytpmuH tup t'ndluoc
together again.

The Language of Jesus

Aramaic, which is closely related to Hebrew, was the language that Jesus spoke. It all but died out in the centuries following Jesus' day. Amazingly, the language still survives today, but only in isolated villages in Syria, Turkey, Iraq, and Iran. Assyrian Christians from northern Iraq still speak it today as well.

A Roll of the Dice

The festival of Purim got its name from a rare word meaning "lot" (Hebrew *pur*). This festival celebrates the reversal of events that had been determined by Haman, the Jews' enemy, by casting lots or dice. An example of such a die, from

Assyria, was found recently, dating to the ninth century B.C. It is a small, six-sided clay cube with the word *pur* on it.

Abracadabra

This word was probably an Aramaic magical word. It was used to ward off fever or inflammation, and, in the Middle Ages, patients were advised to wear it on an amulet to ward off and cure diseases. The word was probably written in this manner:

```
A B R A C A D A B R A
A B R A C A D A B R
A B R A C A D A B
A B R A C A D A
A B R A C A D
A B R A C A
A B R A C
A B R A
A B R
A B
A
```

Dentists in the Bible?

The prophet Amos often used picturesque language to make his point. To illustrate that God had used famine to try to jolt Israel out of its spiritual lethargy, he says that God gave Israel "cleanness of teeth" (Amos 4:6). This is not a reference to personal hygiene, but instead means they had no food to get between their teeth.

You Devil, You!

The word "devil" comes from Greek *diabolos* ("slanderer"), while "Satan" comes from Hebrew *satan* ("adversary"). The New Testament gives us most of our information about the devil, showing him as a malevolent reality, always opposed to God and his people, and whose power will be crushed in the end. He appears in many forms, such as a serpent, a dragon, a sea monster, a flash of lightning, an angel of light, and a roaring lion.

Beelzebub: Lord of the Flies

In William Golding's novel, the lord of the flies was a pig's head worshiped by choirboys-turned-savages. In the Old Testament, Beelzebub was the name of an important Philistine god. In the New Testament, Jesus was accused of driving out demons by the power of Beelzebul (the New Testament word is spelled differently), a reference to Satan, the prince of demons.

The Loch Ness Monster, Too?

Leviathan is a Hebrew name referring to some type of large water creature. In Psalm 104:26, it is clearly a sea creature, possibly a whale or a dolphin. In Job 41:1–34, however, an extended description makes it sound like a crocodile. The Hebrew term was probably deliberately vague, to accommodate all sorts of water monsters.

Hippopotami and Football Players

The Hebrew word *behemoth* is a rare word for "beasts." In Job 40:15, it refers to a large animal, probably the hippopotamus. Many English versions of the bible merely render it as behemoth, however. The modern-day meaning of something large (football players as behemoths) takes its meaning from this passage.

Phoenician Baal

Baal: A God or a Husband?

The Canaanite god Baal is well known in the Bible and in other literature. His name is a generic Semitic word (*baal*) meaning "lord," "master," or "owner." A specialized use of *baal* is "husband," reflecting the idea of husbands as lords over their wives.

The Apple of Your Eye

This phrase is found five times in the King James Version of the Bible, including the prayer "Keep me as the apple of your eye." In reality, the Hebrew word here means "pupil (of the eye)," and the idea is one of God's keeping close watch over his people. Hebrew has a separate word for the fruit.

What Is Anti-Semitic?

The term anti-Semitic today generally means anti-Jewish. The term "Semite" comes from Noah's oldest son Shem, however, and it refers to people who are ethnically (race) or linguistically (language) related to each other. This means that both Jews and Arabs are Semites. It is incorrect then to speak of Arabs as being anti-Semitic.

Ancient Words of Worship

Many Hebrew or Aramaic words are used in modern-day worship. *Hallelujah* means "Praise the Lord!" *Hosanna* was a shout of acclamation used to welcome Jesus into Jerusalem, which originally meant "Save us!" *Amen* is Hebrew for "Surely! So be it!" *Maranatha* was an Aramaic word used by Paul meaning "Our Lord, come!" (referring to hopes of Christ's return to earth).

Prostitutes: "Sacred" and Secular

Hebrew has two words for prostitute. The first refers to cult prostitutes, both male (*qadesh*) and female (*qedeshah*), who were associated with the shrines of various gods. The second word (*zonah*) refers to the more common type.

Creation

The famous poem that begins "Only God can make a tree" obviously wasn't written by an Israelite. The Hebrew language has a special word, *bara,* that refers to God's creative acts. In Hebrew, humans can form, make, and build, and so can God, but only God can create. Since the materials out of which God creates are never mentioned with the word *bara,* we know that God creates out of nothing.

Joseph and His Amazing Technicolor Dream Coat

While this makes a good title for a Broadway musical, and the story of Jacob giving his favorite son a multicolored coat paints a gripping picture, the reference to the coat's color is not necessarily accurate. Most recent Bible versions render the phrase as "a richly ornamented robe," "an ornamented tunic," or "a long robe with sleeves."

The Tale of the Tel

The Hebrew word *tel* refers to a layered mound that has been built up over the centuries by successive occupations. Most large cities in Palestine were rebuilt on the same locations, and the remains of their mounds can still be seen today. The King James Bible's translators had never seen a tel, and thus they mistranslated Joshua 11:13, which refers to "cities that stood on their mounds (tels)" as "cities that stood still in their strength."

Beyond the Pale

This phrase means that something is completely unacceptable or unreasonable, beyond the boundaries of social acceptance. It comes from the Latin word *palus,* meaning "stake," since stakes originally were used in marking the boundaries of Roman military or administrative districts. Famous pales in later periods include the English Pale in

Ireland established in the twelfth century A.D. and the Pale of Settlement in imperial Russia, restricting Jews' rights of settlement.

What's a Parbar?

Many words in the Bible occur only once or twice, and scholars have no real idea what they mean. One modern Bible version, the Revised Standard Version, has this in 1 Chronicles 26:18: "and for the parbar on the west there were four [men] at the road and two at the parbar." It probably means "colonnade" or "court."

Papyrus: Earliest Paper

Papyrus was an early, inexpensive material used as a writing surface. It was made by stripping long papyrus reeds of their bark, laying them next to each other in rows, overlaying them crosswise with more reeds, and then pounding them together. After they dried, a reasonably smooth writing surface was left. Egyptians probably discovered this process. Our word "paper" comes from *papyrus*.

Parchment: Better "Paper"

Parchment is made mainly from the skins of sheep and goats. These skins are soaked in a lime solution, and then the hair and fat are removed by scraping and washing. The skin is stretched on a frame, dried, and then scraped smooth with pumice. Almost all copies of the Bible after the fourth century up until the invention of the printing press were written on parchment, since it is stronger and longer-lasting than papyrus.

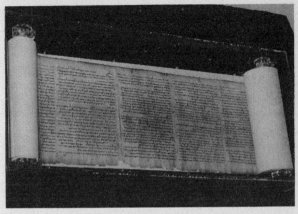

Qumran scroll

Scrolls and Books

Most biblical books were originally written on scrolls, which were sheets of papyrus or parchment sewn or glued together end to end. These were somewhat unwieldy, so books were invented in the early Christian Era. The long scrolls were cut into shorter sheets, and then these were sewn together. The first books (or codexes) were inconveniently sewn together in the center of the page; later ones were sewn along the edges.

An Eye for the Numbers

The Masoretes, the Jewish scribes who painstakingly and meticulously copied the Hebrew Scriptures, were so precise in their copying that they counted the number of words in each book of their Bibles, and even identified the middle word! They did this so they could check themselves and be sure they had not accidentally skipped any words.

Aramaic, the Language of Diplomats

Just as English is the international language of trade and diplomacy (or the *lingua franca*) in most of the world today, so Aramaic was during the time of Israel's monarchy. The Assyrian king Sennacherib's emissaries insulted King Hezekiah's envoys during the siege of Jerusalem by issuing demands in the local language, Hebrew, in full hearing of the common people. This was despite the envoys' request that the negotiations be conducted in Aramaic, for secrecy's sake (2 Kings 18:26–35).

Not All the Old Testament Is in Hebrew

While most of the Old Testament was written in Hebrew, several chapters in Ezra and Daniel (and even one verse in Jeremiah) were written in Aramaic. These sections come in contexts where international affairs are concerned, and the writers felt it advantageous to write in the lingua franca of the day.

Greek in the Holy Land

As ancient Greece rose in power and influence toward the end of the first millennium B.C., so did its language. It was the lingua franca during the time of Jesus. The fact that the New Testament was written in Greek, even though most of its authors were native speakers of Aramaic, attests to the language's influence and vitality.

The Death of Hebrew

Hebrew began to die out as a spoken language
toward the end of the Old Testament period, partly
as a result of the Jews' intermarriage and
assimilation. Nehemiah was distressed to find Jews
who had married foreign women and whose
children could not even speak "the language of
Judah" (Hebrew).

A Living Language

The Hebrew Bible, or Old Testament, was written
over a period of 1,000 years, primarily in Hebrew.
The language changed over that time and
occasionally needed to be updated. One example of
this is in 1 Samuel 9:9: "In times past in Israel, this
is what a man said when he went to inquire of God,
'Come, let us go to the seer.' For what is today
called the prophet used to be called the seer."

How to Write on Clay

A very popular writing surface in ancient times was
wet clay, which was touched with the tip of a
wooden stylus to make wedge-shaped (cuneiform)
impressions. Thousands of such documents have
been uncovered from administrative archives in
ancient cities in the Near East, including Nineveh
and Babylon. Through an accident of history, these
tablets were baked (and thus preserved for posterity)
when cities were destroyed by fire.

The Revival of Hebrew Today

Hebrew was kept alive only among the rabbis in the
synagogues for more than 2,000 years. Then, about

100 years ago, Eliezer Ben-Yehuda, a Lithuanian Jew, proposed and worked tirelessly for its revival as a spoken language. Modern Hebrew is based upon biblical Hebrew and Talmudic Aramaic, and it has traces of Yiddish, German, and Russian.

It's Carved in Stone!

The most important documents in antiquity were laboriously carved into stone, so they were permanent. The Ten Commandments were written on two stone tablets. The Babylonian king Hammurabi's Law Code was written on a hard diorite stone stele.

Balaam's Inscription

In 1967, a dramatic find was made at Tell Deir Alla in the Jordan Valley. A wall inscription dating from the eighth century B.C. mentions the biblical "Balaam son of Beor." The entire text purports to be his own inscription, telling of a night visit he had from the gods. It calls him "a seer of the gods."

The Earliest Greek Writing

A beautiful vase from eighth century B.C. Athens carries the earliest Greek inscription. It was probably a prize won in a contest, for it contains a dedication to "him who dances most delicately."

King Mesha's Inscription

Moabite king Mesha's inscription was carved on a large black basalt stone; it had 34 lines of text. It dates to 830 B.C., and tells of his conflicts with the Israelite kings Omri and Ahab. Mesha says of Omri, "As for Omri, king of Israel, he humbled Moab many years, for Chemosh [the Moabite god] was angry with his land."

The First Hebrew Inscription

The earliest object with a Hebrew text written on it is a limestone tablet containing a farmer's calendar. It was used in Gezer, a biblical city, almost 3,000 years ago. It reads in part:

"His two months are (olive) harvest,
His two months are planting (grain)."

Gezer calendar

Save That Broken Pot!

During Bible times, many short documents were written on *ostraca* (singular: *ostracon*), which were broken pieces of clay bowls or pots. These potsherds were just the right size on which to write a quick letter or note to someone. The writing was done with pen or brush and ink.

A Picture of an Israelite King

The only contemporary pictorial representation of an Israelite king is on the Black Obelisk of the Assyrian king Shalmaneser III. It shows Jehu, king of Israel, on his knees, presenting his tribute of valuable silver and gold items to the Assyrian king.

The Sumerians: The First Literates

The Sumerians, the world's first literate people, lived in the same area as Abraham did years later. The Sumerians composed many texts, including great mythological epics and moving love poetry. One Sumerian text describing a victory of the city of Lagash over the city of Umma is the world's oldest text that uses sequential sentences: It dates from the third millennium B.C.

The Rosetta Stone: Deciphering Hieroglyphics

Egyptian hieroglyphics remained a mystery until Napoleon's troops discovered a large black basalt stone at the Egyptian city of Rosetta in 1799. The stone contained an inscription written in Greek (a known language) and two types of Egyptian writing, one of which was hieroglyphics. It was

deciphered by the French scholar Champollion.
The stone was a decree of King Ptolemy V, who
ruled over Egypt and Palestine in 204 to 180 B.C.

Egyptian Hieroglyphics

When Europeans visited Egypt in the eighteenth
century, they were impressed by its many wonders.
One of those wonders was its mysterious writing
system, which used hieroglyphs ("sacred carvings")
This system used hundreds of colorful pictures as
symbols for words or sounds.

An Egyptian Reference to Israel

The earliest reference to Israel outside the Bible
dates to about 1208 B.C., at a time when Israel had
settled into the land of Canaan after following
Moses out of Egypt. The Egyptian pharaoh
Merneptah boasted in a victory song that he had
defeated many of his enemies, including Israel:
"Israel is laid waste, his seed is not."

Latin: The Language of the Roman Empire and the Church

John 19:20 states that the plaque above Jesus' head
was written in "Hebrew, in Latin, and in Greek."
Hebrew (or Aramaic) was the local language, Greek
was the language of commerce, and Latin was the
language of the Roman Empire. When the Roman
Empire became Christianized in the fourth century
A.D., Latin became the language of the Church. In
the Roman Catholic Church, Latin remained the
language for Mass until the Second Vatican Council
in the 1960s.

The Elephantine Letters

In 1893, the first of several dozen letters written on papyrus and ostraca were found on a small island in the Nile River about 550 miles south of Cairo. A Jewish settlement thrived there in the fifth century B.C. These letters were primarily legal and business texts, but they show the existence of a Jewish temple and that the Jews worshiped many gods.

Ostracon

The Lachish Letters

In 1935 and 1938, a total of 21 letters written on potsherds (ostraca) were found at biblical Lachish, a city about 30 miles southwest of Jerusalem. They are from the two to three years immediately before Jerusalem (and Lachish) fell to the Babylonians in 586 B.C. Most were letters from commanders of military outposts reporting back to the commander in Lachish. They reflect the unsettled conditions of those years.

Jeremiah: Jewish Traitor?

Jeremiah emphasized strongly that the Jews should not resist the Babylonians, since they were God's instrument to punish Judah's sins. Many in Jerusalem, however, did not like this counsel. They accused Jeremiah of being a traitor, saying that "he is weakening the hands of the soldiers who are left in this city" (Jeremiah 38:4). Strikingly, this is precisely the same phrase found in one of the Lachish letters about advice coming from Jerusalem!

The Lights of Azekah

One letter found at Lachish gives a dramatic picture into the rapidly deteriorating situation in the face of the Babylonian assault. The writer informed his commander that they were now watching carefully for the fire signals from Lachish, "for we cannot see Azekah." Azekah was a town about 15 miles north of Lachish that had just fallen to the Babylonians.

The Amarna Letters

An important collection of almost 400 clay tablets was found beginning in 1887 at Tell el-Amarna on the Nile River in Middle Egypt. They date to the middle of the thirteenth century B.C. Most of these were letters from petty kings or their scribes in the land of Canaan to their Egyptian overlords. These show the period to have been one of international diplomacy, but also of constant low-level conflict.

The Nuzi Tablets

More than 4,000 clay tablets were discovered in the 1920s at ancient Nuzi, east of the Tigris River. These date to the middle of the second millennium B.C. These texts give a wide-ranging picture of everyday life at that time, including things such as land ownership, the position of slaves and women, prices and sales of goods, occupations, legal customs, and family law. Many intriguing parallels are found in Genesis and the Nuzi documents.

The Mari Documents

An important cache of almost 20,000 clay tablets was discovered in the 1930s at ancient Mari, on the middle Euphrates River. These were found in the palace of the ancient Babylonian king Zimri-Lim, dating to around 1750 B.C. Among the documents are some 5,000 letters. These come from the land where the biblical patriarchs came from, and date to the time immediately following them.

The Babylonian Chronicles

The Babylonians, in the eighth through sixth centuries B.C., developed a unique type of historical writing called the chronicle. In several important chronicles, the events of each year are listed, along with the king at the time. These are remarkable for their straightforward reporting of the facts, and for their accurate dating, down to the exact year, month, and day.

The Fall of Babylon in a Babylonian Chronicle

The Chronicle of Nabonidus, last king of Babylon, tells of Babylon's fall to the Persian king Cyrus. It is remarkably free of the self-serving rhetoric usually found in such annals. It states that "the army of Cyrus entered Babylon without battle. Afterwards Nabonidus was arrested in Babylon when he returned there.... Cyrus entered Babylon, green twigs were spread in front of him—the state of 'Peace' was imposed upon the city. Cyrus sent greetings to all Babylon."

The Fall of Babylon in a Persian Inscription

King Cyrus of Persia captured Babylon in 539 B.C. His own account of this is much more self-serving than the Babylonian account. Cyrus states that the god Marduk "beheld with pleasure [Cyrus'] good deeds and his upright heart .... Without any battle he made him enter his town Babylon .... All the inhabitants ... bowed to [Cyrus] and kissed his feet... with shining faces. Happily they greeted him as a master ... and they worshiped his very name."

Cyrus' Decree in the Bible

The words of Cyrus' famous decree freeing the Jews from captivity are preserved in Ezra 1:2,3. Cyrus states "The Lord, the God of heaven, has given me all the kingdoms of the earth, and he has charged me to build him a house at Jerusalem.... Whoever is among you of all his people, may his

God be with him, and let him go up to
Jerusalem...and rebuild the house of the Lord, the
God of Israel—he is the God who is in Jerusalem."

Cyrus' Decree in His Own Words

In Cyrus' own royal inscription, he gives the god
Marduk credit for ordering him to allow captive
peoples to return: "I resettled upon the command
of Marduk, the great lord, all the gods...unharmed,
in their former chapels [temples], the places which
make them happy." As a good politician, Cyrus may
well have issued this as a universal decree, and then
issued specific ones to each captive people in which
he mentioned their specific gods.

Ancient Receipts

Many discoveries of ancient texts from Bible lands
have dazzled the public with their dramatic
contents. However, by far the greatest number of
ancient texts are ordinary documents of government
and commerce. For example, a group of 63 ostraca
were found in 1910 at Samaria, dating to the reign
of Jeroboam II. They are mundane receipts, such
as this one: "In the tenth year. From Hazeroth to
Gaddiyahu. A jar of fine oil."

Assyrian Annals

The Assyrian kings developed the custom of
mounting a yearly or every other year military
campaign to conquer new lands. After each
campaign, a record of it was written up. After
several campaigns, several accounts of the first
campaigns existed. It is interesting to note that the

number of enemies killed tend to be progressively inflated in successive editions of these annals.

Shalmaneser, Sargon, and the Fall of Samaria

The Bible tells of the Assyrian king Shalmaneser's conquest of Samaria in 722 B.C., in 2 Kings 17. However, in the Assyrian annals, King Sargon II, Shalmaneser's successor, claims the credit. The problem may be resolved by assuming that Shalmaneser was still king, but his general Sargon actually took the city.

Bombastic Royal Rhetoric

Ancient kings loved to have themselves exalted. Here is how the account of Sennacherib's second military campaign begins: "Sennacherib, the great king, the powerful king…king of the four quarters of the world…wise shepherd, favorite of the great gods, guardian of truth, lover of justice, giver of help, who befriends the weak…a perfect man, a man of war, foremost among all kings…."

Assyrian relief of soldiers

The Fall of Jerusalem

The most traumatic event for Israel in the Old Testament was the destruction of Jerusalem in 586 B.C. by the Babylonians under Nebuchadnezzar (2 Kings 25). The city was razed, the Temple looted and destroyed, most of the people—including the king—carried away into exile, and a puppet ruler set up over the land. Even the great bronze pillars in front of the Temple were carried away.

The Mari Prophets

The documents discovered at Mari in the 1930s contain many "prophecies" delivered by oracular speakers. These are typically messages from the gods to the king, usually with advice about going into battle or not. Compared to biblical prophecy, they are short, trivial, and contain none of the moral dimensions or demands found in the Bible.

A Babylonian Flood Story

Many versions of an ancient flood story exist in the ancient Near East. The most famous tells of a legendary king, Gilgamesh, on a quest for eternal life. Along the way he meets Ut-napishtim, who has been given the gift of immortality by the gods. Ut-napishtim was a hero of old who had survived a flood, like Noah, by building a boat. Many details are similar to the biblical flood story.

Caveat Emptor!
("Let the Buyer Beware!")

A charming candor can be found in some of the Mari prophecies about the reliability or urgency of the prophecy. These are usually reported in a letter to the king, and several conclude with the letter's author telling the king that he may "take it or leave it." The following phrase is typical: "Let my lord do what pleases him [concerning this prophecy]." It is difficult to imagine biblical prophets saying similar things.

Hymn to the Moon God

Almost every ancient people produced hymns to their gods. Here is part of a Sumerian-Akkadian hymn to Sin, the moon god: "O Father…in the heavens, who is exalted?…You alone are exalted. On earth, who is exalted?… You alone are exalted…. O king of kings, exalted one, whose office no one can rival, whose divinity no god can equal…. May your beloved wife Ningal, the gracious, say to you, 'Rest, O Lord.'"

Hymn to the Nile

For the Egyptians, the Nile River was their lifeline, and so its gods were among the highest in the Egyptian pantheon. Here is part of a hymn to the Nile: "Hail to thee, O Nile, that issues from the earth and comes to keep Egypt alive!… The bringer of food, rich in provisions, creator of all good, lord of majesty, sweet in fragrance."

In Praise of Scribes

To be a scribe was a noble aspiration in the ancient Near East, especially in Egypt. Several compositions praise this profession. The following is a good example: "[The scribes] did not make for themselves pyramids of metal, with tombstones there of iron. They were not able to leave heirs in children...pronouncing their names, but they made heirs for themselves in the writings and in the books of wisdom which they composed."

Proverbs and the Wisdom of Amen-em-Opet

The close ties between Proverbs and some Egyptian wisdom can be seen in the following quotes:
Amen-em-Opet:
"Guard thyself against robbing the oppressed
And against overbearing the disabled."
"Do not associate to thyself the heated man,
Nor visit him for conversation."
Proverbs:
"Do not rob the poor, because he is poor,
or crush the afflicted at the gate" (Proverbs 22:22).
"Make no friendship with a man given to anger,
nor go with a wrathful man" (Proverbs 22:24).

A Strange Famine

The prophet Amos gives a startlingly vivid picture of what conditions would soon be like in Israel, because of its rejection of the Lord: "I will send a famine on the land; not a famine of bread... but of hearing the words of the Lord.... they shall run to and fro, to seek the word of the Lord, but they shall not find it" (Amos 8:11,12).

The Writing of God

The Bible claims to be the word of God. However, some passages mention God's writing explicitly. The Ten Commandments were "written with the

Moses and the Ten Commandments

finger of God" (Exodus 31:18); they were "the writing of God" (Exodus 32:16). The pattern for the Temple is described as "the writing from the hand of the Lord" (1 Chronicles 28:19).

A Strange Meal

On two occasions, biblical characters ate a scroll that contained God's words as a symbol of internalizing them: the prophet Ezekiel (Ezekiel 2:8–3:3) and also the Apostle John (Revelation 10:9,10). In both cases it tasted "sweet as honey," which echoes the words of Psalm 119:103: "How sweet are thy words to my taste, sweeter than honey to my mouth!"

113

Book Burning

The Bible records two occasions on which books were burned. King Jehoiakim of Judah burned the Book of Jeremiah strip by strip as it was read to him (Jeremiah 36:23). A number of magicians at Ephesus, who were converted as a result of Paul's preaching, brought their books of magic together and burned them publicly (Acts 19:19).

Heavenly Books

In many passages, the Bible refers to books kept in heaven. Moses pleads with God to blot him out of the "book which you have written" (Exodus 32:32) for the sake of Israel's forgiveness. A psalmist asks God to "put thou my tears in thy bottle! Are they not in thy book?" (Psalm 56:8). The books of Daniel and Revelation both speak of the day that "the books were opened" (Daniel 7:10 and Revelation 20:12). Daniel refers to the "book of truth" (Daniel 10:21). The Book of Malachi speaks of a "book of remembrance" that was written about those who feared the Lord (Malachi 3:16).

And the Students Said, "Amen!"

The author of Ecclesiastes voiced the complaints of endless generations of students when he said, "Of making many books there is no end, and much study is a weariness of the flesh" (Ecclesiastes 12:12). His point was that fearing God and pleasing him are what bring true fulfillment.

The Book of Life

The most commonly mentioned heavenly book is the Book of Life. It refers to the keeping of an account of those who are truly believers and those who are not. In Revelation, those whose names are found written in the Book of Life will escape the everlasting judgment. Most other heavenly books are related to the Book of Life in some way.

The House of the Archives

Jewish leaders once sent a request to the Persian king to search the royal archives for records that could clarify a local conflict. The king did, and found the relevant documents in "the house of the archives where the documents were stored." Every major empire had a vast bureaucracy supported by thousands of legal and administrative documents. Most excavations of ancient cities have uncovered royal archives with valuable troves of such documents.

A Bible for the Commoner

The New Testament was written in the language of the common person. This style is called *koine* Greek, meaning "common," "everyday." It contrasts sharply with the sophisticated and complex Greek of Athens, called Attic Greek. This meant that the New Testament could be read and understood by the vast majority of people throughout the Mediterranean world.

Familiar Greek Words

Many English words have their roots in Greek words used in the New Testament. *Theos* ("God") and *logos* ("word," "study") yields theology (the study of God). *Megalo* ("great") and *polis* ("city") yield megalopolis (huge metropolitan area). *Ekklesia* ("church") yields ecclesiastical (having to do with the church). *Anthropos* ("man") yields anthropology (the study of man). *Angelos* is "angel"; *ethnosis* is "nation"; *proselutos* is "proselyte"; *baptizo* is "baptize"; *meter* is "mother"; *pater* is "father."

All Sins Are Forgiven!

Psalm 32 is a beautiful reflection on the joys of having one's sins forgiven. It uses no less than four words for sin in its opening lines: "Happy are those whose *transgression* is forgiven, whose *sin is* covered. Happy are those to whom the Lord imputes no *iniquity,* and in whose spirit there is no *deceit.*" The variety of terms used creates the solid assurance that whatever the sin is, it is covered and forgiven.

Stammering Barbarians

Our word "barbarian" comes from the Greek *barbaros,* which referred to a foreigner, someone speaking an unintelligible language. It is found in Romans 1:14, referring to non-Greeks. The word arose to imitate the way a foreign tongue sounded to Greek ears, a stammering, unknown sound. Originally, the word had no insulting connotation at all.

Philistine Behavior

The word philistine has come to mean uncultured or boorish in English. This is because of the mostly negative presentation of the Philistines in the Bible, who were Israel's major enemy between 1150 to 1000 B.C. The Philistine culture, however, was fairly advanced in political organization and especially in the arts.

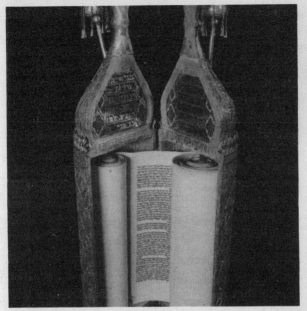

Torah scroll

Studying Torah and Shooting Arrows

The Hebrew verb that is related to the noun Torah is *yarah,* which means "to shoot an arrow." The relationship between the two is that the Torah points in the right direction, aims toward the mark of a right relationship with God. Interestingly enough, one of the major words for sin in Hebrew (*chata*) means "to miss the mark."

What Is a Helpmate?

This usually refers to a wife, in her role as helper to her husband. The word has arisen from the King

James Version's rendering of two Hebrew words in Genesis 2:18, where God says, "I will make [Adam] an help meet for him." However, "meet" in seventeenth-century English meant "appropriate," "fit for." So, helpmate was not originally a true word; modern versions usually translate the phrase "a helper fit for him."

What Does Bar Mitzvah Mean?

Bar is Aramaic for "son" and *mitzvah* is Hebrew for "commandment"; hence, the term means "son of the commandment." It is applied in the Talmud to every adult male, denoting "a man of duty."

What Is a Bar Mitzvah Celebration?

The custom of a Bar Mitzvah celebration arose only a few centuries ago. It takes place when a boy reaches his thirteenth birthday, at which time he ranks as an adult and is held responsible for his own religious life. The boy reads a portion of the Torah and usually expounds on a religious topic at a public celebration. The custom of a Bat Mitzvah for girls (*bat* means "daughter") has arisen recently in some branches of Judaism.

A Biblical Airhead?

Jesus spoke about empty-headed people when he said, "Anyone who says to his brother 'Raca,' is answerable to the Sanhedrin" (Matthew 5:22). The Aramaic word is one of insult, related to the Hebrew term for empty. It means something like empty-headed one (our modern-day translation might be airhead or blockhead).

The Salt Covenant

Salt was a seasoning to be offered with Israelite sacrifices, and covenants were sealed with sacrificial meals where salt was present. Since salt was also a preservative, a "salt covenant" symbolized eternity. This first referred to the holy offerings due the priests and Levites in perpetuity (Numbers 18:19), and later the eternal kingship that God had given David and his sons (2 Chronicles 13:5).

An Eye for an Eye

The penalties stated in Exodus 21:23–25 concerning an eye for an eye or a life for a life may sound barbaric to many people today. However, the principle was a very humane one: Let the punishment fit the crime. This limited the usual cycle of escalating retribution and revenge.

Paul's Thorn in the Flesh

The Apostle Paul mentioned a "thorn in the flesh" that was given him to keep him from pride (2 Corinthians 12:7). He asked God three times about it, but it was never removed. Scholars have speculated almost endlessly about what it was. Suggestions include earaches, headaches, eye afflictions, epilepsy, hysteria, malaria, speech impediment, sexual lust, or human enemies. We do not know what his problem was.

The Canaanites: Israel's Thorn in Its Sides

When Israel inherited the land of Canaan, one of its top priorities was to drive out the Canaanites, who worshiped many pagan gods. God repeatedly warned them of the dangers of mixing with them. At one point, he stated that they would be "as pricks in your eyes and thorns in your sides" (Numbers 33:55).

Chariots of the Sun

King Josiah removed the "horses that the kings of Judah had dedicated to the sun" from the entrance to the Temple, and he burned their "chariots of the sun" with fire as part of his great reform movement to rid Israel of all foreign gods and follow only God (2 Kings 23:11). Worship of the sun god was common in the ancient Near East, and several cultures depicted him as a charioteer riding across the sky pulling the sun behind him.

An Archaic Word: *Neesing*

Job 41 describes a creature called Leviathan that many scholars believe is the crocodile. Parts of the description make it sound like a dragon. Here is the King James Version of verse 18: "By his neesings a light doth shine." *Neesing* was the seventeenth-century word for "sneezing."

666: The Number of the Beast

The beast's number is 666 (Revelation 13:18). This has led to endless speculation about the beast's identity. Some people have used various methods of assigning numbers to letters to try to find out who the beast is. Many early interpreters thought individual Roman emperors were being referred to. Irenaeus (and many modern interpreters) saw the number as symbolic of all evil. Being one digit short of the triple number of perfection—777—it symbolizes evil's perversion and falling short of the true standard of perfection.

Jesus preaches the Sermon on the Mount.

Casting Pearls Before Swine

In the Sermon on the Mount, Jesus said "Do not give dogs what is holy; and do not throw your pearls before swine." Holy things and pearls here

121

represent the truths of the Gospel, and dogs and pigs—despised animals in Scripture—represent any people who have become cynical and hardened against God's word. The saying emphasized the importance of choosing how and where to preach the Gospel.

The Unfathomable Chemistry of Love

Among the proverbs of Agur in Proverbs 30 is a list of four things he does not understand: "the way of an eagle in the sky, the way of a serpent on a rock, the way of a ship on the high seas, and the way of a man with a maiden" (verse 19).

Abraham's Bosom

The old Negro spiritual that said "Rock'a my soul in the bosom of Abraham" spoke of a place of comfort and security. The phrase comes from Luke 16:22,23, in Jesus' parable about Lazarus. When Lazarus died, he was carried by the angels to "Abraham's bosom," the place of high honor and intimacy.

Beautiful Feet

The prophet Isaiah painted an exquisite word picture of comfort for Jerusalem when he stated: "How beautiful on the mountains are the feet of the one who brings—who announces peace, who brings good news, who announces salvation, who says to Zion, 'Your God reigns!'" (Isaiah 52:7). The focus on the feet of the messenger adds to the impact of the uplifting message. The Apostle Paul used this passage to encourage people to preach the Gospel (Romans 10:15).

The Calves of Our Lips

In Hosea 14:2, the King James Version states that God's people would respond to his grace by offering "the calves of our lips." Most modern versions have "the fruit of our lips" (meaning praises to God). The Hebrew can be paraphrased as "we shall offer the praise of our lips in place of sacrificial bullocks." This means that praise, not sacrifice, is the valued offering.

Humpty Dumpty and the Apostle Paul

In a famous passage in Lewis Carroll's *Through the Looking Glass,* Humpty Dumpty says, "When I use a word, it means just what I choose it to mean— neither more nor less." The Apostle Paul wasn't quite this cavalier, but he did take certain Greek words and give them new meanings or nuances. This was often necessary because classical Greek did not have ways of expressing the great theological truths he wanted to explain.

Mammon

This word comes from an Aramaic term (*mamona*) meaning "wealth." Jesus gave negative connotations to the term when he said "You cannot serve God and mammon" (Matthew 6:24) and when he referred to "unrighteous mammon" (Luke 16:9,11). The latter term probably referred to ill-gotten gains. The point in both of these cases is as G. B. Caird said, "All money, however acquired, is tainted unless used in God's service."

"Red Sky at Night, Sailor's Delight"

Boy and Girl Scouts often learn such sayings to help them survive in the outdoors. However, such wisdom is not new. People knew this in Jesus' day. He once told a group of Jewish leaders, "When it is evening, you say, 'It will be fair weather; for the sky is red.' And in the morning, 'It will be stormy today, for the sky is red and threatening' " (Matthew 16:2,3).

Love By Any Other Name

The Greek language has three major words for love. The first (*eros*) denotes sexual love. This word was common in classical Greek, but is never found in the New Testament. The second (*philos*) denotes married love or a close friendship. The third (*agape*) was rarely used in classical Greek, but it is the most common word for love in the New Testament. The biblical writers used it to describe God's love.

Theopneustos: A New Word

An example where Paul actually invented a new word is *Theopneustos,* which means "God-breathed." This is formed by combining *Theos* ("God") and *pneuma* ("breath"). The word was not used in Paul's day, but he coined the term to describe the nature of Scripture: It was "God-breathed," meaning the very words of God (2 Timothy 3:16). Usually *Theopneustos* is translated "inspired by God."

The Sign of Jonah

When the Pharisees and Sadducees asked Jesus for a sign, he refused, except to refer them to "the sign

Jonah swallowed by the big fish.

of the prophet Jonah" (Matthew 12:39). Just as Jonah had been in the fish's belly for three days and nights, so Jesus would be in the grave for the same amount of time. Jesus' appearance after the three days would indict his generation, just as Jonah's appearance in Nineveh after three days indicted the Ninevites.

"Get Behind Me, Satan"

This is the sharp rebuke Jesus directed at Peter when he was speaking of the suffering that Jesus was to undergo, and Peter objected that this should not occur (Matthew 16:23). The effect of Peter's words were to tempt Jesus to abandon his mission, and he rebuked Peter in similar terms that he had done earlier with Satan himself (Matthew 4:10). The phrase today is usually used in a joking manner, when innocent temptations arise.

"Be Strong! Be Strong!"

God encouraged Joshua by telling him "Be strong and very courageous!" (Joshua 1:6,7,9). In Jewish tradition, after any of the five Books of Moses is read publicly in the synagogue, the congregation rises and proclaims "Be strong! Be strong! And let us take courage!" This refers to the courage to live according to the teachings in these books.

What Does *Selah* Mean?

Selah is a Hebrew term found 71 times in the Book of Psalms and three times in a psalm in Habakkuk. It usually comes at the end of a poetic stanza. Scholars do not know its exact meaning, but it is probably a musical or liturgical instruction of some type, such as pause or crescendo.

Speaking in Tongues

On the day of Pentecost, Jesus' followers were together in a house when a mighty wind rushed upon them, flames of fire rested on each of them, and they each began to "speak in tongues" (in languages they did not know). Jews from many different countries were in Jerusalem at the time, and each heard Jesus' followers speaking in their own language. This was a sign of the Holy Spirit's presence.

A Grim Double Entendre

A double entendre is a word or phrase with a double meaning. In Genesis 40, Joseph tells Pharaoh's butler in prison that Pharaoh will "lift up your head and restore you." He tells Pharaoh's baker that Pharaoh will "lift up your head—from you!—and hang you on a tree."

Through a Glass Darkly

The Apostle Paul spoke of heavenly things using this eloquent phrase. He said that we perceive heavenly things imperfectly, as "through a glass, darkly, but then face to face" (1 Corinthians 13:12). Modern versions speak of seeing in a mirror dimly, but the point is the same.

What's That Log Doing in Your Eye?

Jesus used hyperbole and figurative language very effectively when he scolded people for noticing specks or splinters in other people's eyes while ignoring the logs in their own eyes (Matthew 7:3–5). His point was to condemn hypocrisy.

Whitewashed Tombs

A striking metaphor that Jesus used was to compare the Pharisees with whitewashed tombs to show their hypocrisy. On the outside, many of them were freshly painted and clean, but on the inside they were full of dead bones and all manner of uncleanness (Matthew 23:27).

Am I My Brother's Keeper?

This is the response of Cain—who killed his brother Abel—when God came to him and asked him where Abel was (Genesis 4:9). He was attempting to deflect or escape responsibility for his crime. The phrase is often used today by people wanting to avoid responsibility or to claim they are not responsible for certain things.

Who Was Belial?

Belial was not originally a name, but it developed into a name for Satan in Jewish literature in the period between the Testaments. The Apostle Paul used the word in this way when he asked "What accord has Christ with Belial?" (2 Corinthians 6:15).

How Do You Raise Ebenezer?

A well-known hymn written in the eighteenth century and still in use today contains the line "Here I raise mine Ebenezer." *Ebenezer* is a Hebrew term meaning "stone of help." After a victory over the Philistines, Samuel set up a memorial stone and called it Ebenezer because the Lord had helped Israel.

Physician, Heal Thyself

This was a skeptical challenge that Jesus predicted the people from his hometown would hurl at him when he tried to do miracles there. It could be paraphrased as follows: You heal others so well, let's see you heal yourself. Jesus called it a proverb, indicating that it must have been a common phrase. The attitude it expresses is "you have done so well elsewhere, let's see you do the same here."

Nothing New Under the Sun

The author of Ecclesiastes uses the phrase "under the sun" more than 25 times, as he expresses a weariness with life. In his search for fulfillment, he discovers that: "What has been is what will be, and what has been done is what will be done; and there is nothing new under the sun" (Ecclesiastes 1:9). He concludes that the search for something new is misguided, that fulfillment comes in fearing God.

Turning the Other Cheek

In Jesus' Sermon on the Mount, he spoke in detail about ethical living. He stated that if someone "strikes you on the right cheek, turn to him the other also" (Matthew 5:39). This made the point about not seeking revenge for injury, but forgiving wrongdoers.

The Sermon on the Mount

Jesus and the U.S. Marines

The United States Marine Corps had a recruiting slogan that said they were looking for "a few good men." This is similar to Jesus' words about the relatively few people who actually would respond to his invitation to salvation—"many are called, but few are chosen" (Matthew 22:14). The major difference is that the Marines' invitation is selective, while Jesus' is inclusive.

From Dust to Dust

"Ashes to ashes, dust to dust" are words often spoken at the gravesite during a funeral. The term is adapted from God's words to Adam in Genesis 3:19, reminding him that he was formed out of the ground and would return there: "you are dust, and to dust you shall return."

Blood Money

When Judas Iscariot betrayed Jesus to the Jewish authorities, Judas was given 30 pieces of silver in payment. This has led to the phrase "blood money," which is money received in exchange for the life of a human being.

Swing Low, Sweet Chariot?

The old Negro spiritual by this title speaks (mistakenly) of the chariot that will take the believer home (to heaven). The image comes from 2 Kings 2:11, where Elijah was taken into heaven by a fiery chariot and fiery horses. However, the text actually says that Elijah was taken up in a whirlwind, not in the chariot itself.

Elijah is taken to heaven.

Chariots of Fire

The Academy-Award-winning movie *Chariots of Fire* took its name from a biblical image, which was appropriate, since it was a story about a committed Christian runner. The image comes from 2 Kings 2:11, where a chariot of fire and horses of fire appeared and the prophet Elijah was taken up into heaven. Isaiah 66:15 also mentions the Lord coming angrily in chariots of fire to judge the earth.

The Abomination of Desolation

Daniel 11 speaks of the rise of Antiochus Epiphanes, the ruler of the Seleucid Empire, and of his profaning of the Temple in Jerusalem in 168 B.C. He is a "contemptible person" (verse 21), and he will set up "an abomination of desolation" (verse 31). The books of 1 and 2 Maccabees detail this desecration. Jesus predicted that another "desolating sacrilege" would be set up in Jerusalem at the end of the age.

Thirty Pieces of Silver

The price paid to Judas for Jesus was 30 pieces of silver. This was a ridiculously low sum. In the Old Testament, this was the sum to be paid if a man's ox gored a slave. This reflects the low esteem in which Jesus was held by Judas and the Jewish leaders.

Faith, Hope, and Love

Paul's great reflections on love are found in 1 Corinthians 13. At the end of his discussion, he stresses that "faith, hope, and love" are the greatest of all gifts, but he concludes that "the greatest of these is love."

Rolling Away in Gilgal

The first place the Israelites encamped in the land of Canaan after they had crossed the Jordan River was Gilgal. Here they circumcised all males, since they had neglected this practice in the wilderness. They named the site "Gilgal" in a word-play on the reproach of Egypt that was finally rolled away (Joshua 5:9). The Hebrew word for "to roll" is *galal*.

What or Where Is *Sheol?*

The Hebrew term sheol occurs 65 times in the Old Testament, referring to the place of the dead. The King James Version translates it "hell" 31 times, the "grave" 31 times, and the "pit" 3 times. While it means merely the grave at times, sometimes it seems to refer more to a shadowy realm of the dead. The full-blown concept of hell as a place of punishment is not developed in the Old Testament.

Hell

This English word comes from an old Germanic word meaning "hidden place." The King James Version translates several words as hell: sheol, hades, and gehenna. The last of these is the most proper source for hell, however. In the New Testament, the idea of hell as eternal punishment is found in its full expression. It is accompanied by fiery imagery ("a lake of fire"), and its location is a nebulous place under the earth.

Animals on the Ark

All the animals did not enter the ark two by two, as is commonly thought. God told Noah to take seven pairs of all clean animals. These were the animals approved for eating by Hebrew dietary laws. Noah was also to take one pair of all the other unclean animals and seven pairs of the birds of the air.

"Animals Enter the Ark" by James J. Tissot

Jonah and the big fish

A Whale of a Tale?

Contrary to popular belief, Jonah was probably not swallowed by a whale. Jonah's fateful journey was in the Mediterranean, where whales are rarely sighted today and may have been unknown in biblical times. The Bible merely mentions a "great fish" and a "large sea monster" as Jonah's seaworthy refuge.

"Baboons! But I Ordered Peacocks!"

Every three years, King Solomon's fleet of trading ships brought back many riches, including "baboons," according to the New International Version, or "peacocks," according to the New Revised Standard Version. The Hebrew word is either related to the Egyptian word for baboon or the Tamil (Indian) word for peacock.

Biblical Animals

The Bible mentions dozens of animals, wild and domestic, in many different contexts. Almost 180 Hebrew terms exist for animals, and more than 50 Greek terms. Unfortunately, not all the terms can be identified with certainty, and many animals have become extinct since biblical times.

Unicorns in the Bible?

The King James Version of the Bible mentions unicorns nine times. The actual animal is the oryx, a magnificent white horselike creature with two long, straight horns. It was hunted almost to extinction in the nineteenth century. Today, it is slowly being restored in Israel by wildlife conservationists.

Animals and Humans

Genesis 1 and 2 tell us that God created animals before humans, that he gave humans responsibility to be good stewards over the animals, and that Adam gave names to them. Originally, humans were vegetarians, but after Noah's flood, God gave animals for food as well. Animals served humans as sources of food, for transportation, in working the fields, as sacrificial animals, in the military, and as pets.

Jezebel is eaten by dogs.

Dogs

In Israel, dogs ran loose and lived as scavengers. They were despised and considered unclean by the Israelites. Proverbs 26:11 mentions a dog returning to its vomit, and, in one gruesome episode, the wicked queen Jezebel's body was eaten by dogs in the street after her death. Some dogs were kept as sheep dogs though, and some may even have been household pets in some lands.

Cats

Cats are mentioned only in the apocrypal Letter of Jeremiah (verse 22). This verse speaks of bats, swallows, birds, and cats alighting with impunity on the heads of idols, which shows that the idols are not gods. Cats were sacred in Egypt, and their mummies were preserved by the thousands. They were domesticated in Egypt for catching rodents, since large scale grain storage was practiced, but they were not kept in Palestine.

Camels

The camel is an ideal desert beast of burden, since it has an extraordinary ability to go long periods of time without water. Because of its ungainly looks, some people joke that it is a horse put together by committee. The camel was domesticated about 3000 B.C., but it was not commonly used until the twelfth century B.C. We get our word "camel" from the Hebrew word *gamal*.

Donkeys

Donkeys are mentioned frequently in the Bible. The donkey was one of the basic possessions of the ordinary Hebrew family. It was used for powering machinery to grind corn, for pulling simple plows, and for riding. It was an unclean animal, and thus not to be eaten, although during a siege of Samaria, a donkey's head was sold for food at a very high price (2 Kings 6:25).

Balaam's donkey sees an angel.

Balaam's Donkey

Balaam holds the dubious distinction of being the
only biblical character to have had a conversation
with a donkey. Balaam was an enigmatic
Mesopotamian prophet and magician who was
hired by Balak, an enemy of Israel, to curse Israel.
On his way there, his donkey balked at going on
because it saw an angel and was fearful. The donkey
even spoke to Balaam about what he saw, according
to Numbers 22:28–30.

Kings and Donkeys

Several passages in the Old Testament speak of a
king riding on a donkey. This is most striking in
Zechariah 9:9, where it is prophesied that a king
comes triumphant and victorious yet riding humbly
on a donkey (and chariots and war-horses are
mentioned in the next verse). Jesus' entrance into

Jerusalem on a donkey fulfilled this prophecy (Matthew 21:5). The use of a donkey instead of a horse emphasized the peaceful nature of the king.

Unequally Yoked Animals

It was common in ancient times (as well as modern times) to yoke an ox and a donkey together to pull a plow. However, the Mosaic Law prohibited this (Deuteronomy 22:10). While this may have been for its moral lesson, it also was humane, since the animals were not well matched for joint work.

Oxen

Several words in Hebrew are translated variously as cattle, bulls, oxen, etc. Oxen are castrated adult bulls. They were used in biblical lands as sacrificial animals, for plowing and other agricultural uses, and they provided hides and meat as well. They are thought to have originated with the wild ox, which many scholars think was the aurochs, an animal that is now extinct.

Cattle

Many different words were used to represent cattle, including herd, heifer, bull, calf, and ox. Cattle were kept in great numbers in biblical lands, and they were symbols of wealth. The cattle provided milk, meat, leather, manure (fuel for cooking), and horns, and they were also used as draft animals and for sacrifices.

Bulls

Bulls were symbols of strength in most cultures in the ancient Near East. As such, they came to be objects of worship. Typically, the highest of the gods were represented as having bull-like features. Bulls adorned royal thrones, palaces, and temples. The Israelites fell prey to bull worship, building golden bull calves on at least two occasions.

The Nativity

"Away in a Manger"

The Gospel of Luke mentions the manger into which Jesus was laid when he was born (Luke 2:7). Most scholars think this was a feeding trough for cattle. Excavations at Megiddo and Lachish, towns of the Old Testament period, have uncovered stone feeding troughs of this type. St. Jerome stated that Jesus' manger was made of mud or clay, which may be true given the scarcity of wood and the difficulty of hewing out stone.

Sheep

Hebrew has some 12 different words for sheep, such as ram, lamb, ewe, and flock. This undoubtedly reflects the important place sheep had in Israelite life and economy in Old Testament times. Sheep were the most common animals to be sacrificed. Both the Old and New Testaments refer often to sheep symbolically as innocent, helpless, docile, or sacrificial animals. One of the best-known verses is in the beloved Psalm 23, which begins, "The Lord is my shepherd, I shall not want."

Lice

The third plague on the Egyptians was the plague of lice, according to several Bible versions (some versions say maggots or gnats). Lice were a common problem in the ancient world, and the ancients fashioned beautiful combs to deal with the problem. Archaeologists have found the remains of lice and their eggs in combs at many sites.

Lambs

Lambs are almost exclusively symbolic in the Bible. They represented innocence and gentleness. God's care for his people was often expressed in terms of a shepherd watching over his lambs. Unblemished lambs were to be sacrificed for people's sins, and Jesus is called the Lamb of God, referring to his status as an innocent who was sacrificed for the world's sins.

Goats

Goats were kept for their milk, the meat of the kid, and for sacrificial purposes. Goatskins were used for carrying liquids, and the goat's long hair was used in making cloth. Seventy percent of the Bible's references to goats are as animals for sacrifice, although sheep were more commonly used. Jesus mentioned that all people would be separated into the sheep (favored) and the goats (condemned) at the final judgment.

Locusts

The eighth plague on Egypt was an incredible swarm of locusts, and the books of Joel and Revelation depict locusts as God's instruments of judgment. Even in modern times, swarms of locusts have darkened the skies and devastated areas up to 400 square miles wide.

Snakes: Threats to Life

Snakes are mentioned in the Bible mostly as symbols, usually as threats. Evil entered the world through Satan in the form of a snake (Genesis 3), and wicked people are often compared to snakes or their venom. The threat of great harm is often compared to a snakebite. The craftiness of snakes also is mentioned, as Jesus told his disciples to be wise as serpents and innocent as doves.

Snakes

The Bible has seven or eight words for snakes. Occasionally, snakes are mentioned in actual historical episodes, such as the serpents that attacked the Israelites in the wilderness (Numbers 21) or the snake that bit the Apostle Paul on the island of Malta (Acts 28).

Snake Handlers

Mark 16 states that just before Jesus returned to heaven, he told his followers that they would have new powers because of their faith: They would be able to cast out demons, speak in new languages, handle deadly snakes, and drink poison with no harm. Some eccentric Christian groups today, mainly in Appalachia, take this to mean that all Christians must do this, and they handle snakes and drink poisons as part of their religious rituals.

Fish

Fish were an abundant source of food in all Bible lands. The Law of Moses (Deuteronomy 14:9,10) allowed eating "whatever has fins and scales" (most fish), but it prohibited eating whatever did not have these (thus excluding sharks, eels, and rays, and water mammals, reptiles, and invertebrates). The Israelites, as well as Jesus and his disciples, regularly ate fish.

The Symbolism of Fish

Fish and fishing are mentioned symbolically many times in the Bible. Usually the imagery has to do with catching fish, whether with nets or otherwise.

Jesus calls his disciples.

Amos' prophecy about Samaria's doom is jarring: "they shall take you away with hooks, even the last of you with fishhooks" (Amos 4:2). Jesus spoke of making his disciples "fishers of men" (Matthew 4:19). Deuteronomy 4:18 prohibited the making of any image of a fish.

Saint Peter's Fish

Jesus told his disciple Peter to go fish in the
Sea of Galilee, predicting that the first fish he
caught would have a shekel coin in its mouth
(Matthew 17:24–27). Peter was then to take this
shekel and pay his and Jesus' taxes with it. The fish
was probably the Tilapia, a fish found in the Sea of
Galilee. This fish has a large mouth in which it
carries its eggs, and it is often called St. Peter's Fish.

Jesus' Sponge

Roman soldiers gave Jesus a drink from a sponge
while he was on the cross. Sponges are marine
animals whose skeletons provide the familiar
sponge. The Roman writer Pliny states that it was
standard practice for Roman soldiers to carry a
sponge with them to use in getting themselves a
drink, precisely in the way that the Gospels
describe.

Bees

The Bible mentions bees a number of times. Twice
the swarming habits of honeybees are mentioned:
Psalm 118:12 says that "[The nations] surrounded
me like bees," while Deuteronomy 1:44 mentions
the Amorites chasing the Israelites like bees. Samson
encountered a swarm of honeybees in the carcass of
a lion (Judges 14:8). The Hebrew word for "bee" is
deborah.

Hornets

Three times the Bible mentions that God sent
swarming hornets ahead of the Israelites into the

land of Canaan to drive out their enemies. Some scholars see this as a literal reference to hornets, while others see it as a symbol of Egypt, just as the fly and the bee are symbols of Egypt and Assyria in Isaiah 7:18. Others see it as a symbol of God's direct intervention, which paralized the enemy.

Crocodile Wrestling

Job 41 tells of the crocodile's mighty power as follows: "Lay hands on him; think of the battle; you will not do it again!" (verse 8). It describes the crocodile's snout and skin this way: "Who can strip off his outer garment? Who can penetrate his coat of mail? Who can open the doors of his face? Round about his teeth is terror. His back is made of rows of shields ...." (verses 13–15).

Scorpions

Scorpions are mentioned many times in the Bible, always as threats the Israelites faced or as symbols of great pain and hardship. Jesus appointed 70 followers to whom he gave authority to "tread upon serpents and scorpions...and nothing shall hurt you" (Luke 10:19).

Crocodiles

Crocodiles were abundant in the Nile River in biblical times, although not elsewhere. An entire chapter in Job is devoted to describing the crocodile, called "Leviathan" (Job 41). The chapter contains a series of rhetorical questions to Job about what he can do to the awesome crocodile (answer: nothing). This makes the point that God created even this fearsome creature. The descriptions in this chapter are surprisingly detailed.

Lizards

Leviticus 11:29–30 mentions several animals that are unclean, most of them reptiles related to the lizard. They include "the great lizard...the gecko, the land crocodile, the lizard, the sand lizard, and the chameleon." These all were among the "swarming things that swarm upon the earth." Lizards were (and are) common in Palestine.

Birds

The Bible mentions some 50 types of birds. More than 350 species of birds are identified today in Palestine. Birds are included among sacrificial animals and among clean (edible) and unclean animals. They figure in numerous stories in the Bible (the doves and raven of Noah's ark). Their habits and nesting places are referred to often in prophetic and poetic literature.

Falcons

The falcon is a bird of prey. About ten species are known from Palestine. In Leviticus 11:14, falcons are mentioned as an abomination, not to be eaten. Job 28:7 speaks of their keen vision. One of the highest Egyptian gods was Horus, a falcon-god.

Ostriches

The ostrich was common in biblical lands, but today it is extinct there. It was used for food and for its feathers, and it is occasionally depicted in the art of Egypt and Assyria. Ornamental cups made from ostrich eggshells have been found in Assyrian graves from about 3000 B.C. Ostriches are described in considerable detail in Job 39:13–18, where their reputation for cruelty and stupidity is mentioned, as well as their blinding speed.

Owls

No less than eight species of owls have been tentatively identified from the lists of unclean birds in Leviticus and Deuteronomy, including the eagle owl, short- and long-eared owls, wood owl, fisher owl, screech owl, little owl, and scops owl. The eagle owl is the world's largest, measuring up to 28 inches long. A beautiful sandy-colored desert variety is known from Palestine.

Ravens

The raven is the largest member of the crow family, and it is first encountered in the story of Noah's flood (Genesis 8:7). It was one of the unclean animals (Leviticus 11:15). God's care for the raven was a symbol of his care for his people, and it also was a symbol of judgment and desolation.

Hoopoes

The hoopoe is mentioned only twice, in the lists of abominations in Leviticus 11:19 and Deuteronomy 14:18. It is a beautiful bird, but it is filthy in its eating and nesting habits. Also, it was a sacred bird to the Egyptians. These facts probably account for its prohibition in Israel. It has spectacular plumage. Its beak is long, thin, and curved.

The dove returns to the ark with an olive branch.

Doves and Pigeons

Doves and pigeons were the most important birds in the Old Testament. They were used often in sacrifices. When pigeons were used, they were always "young pigeons" (see Leviticus 1:14). Noah sent out three doves from the ark to find land; the second brought back an olive leaf, a symbol of new

151

life. Jesus talked about doves to symbolize guiltlessness when he said "be wise as serpents and innocent as doves" (Matthew 10:16).

Roosters

The common cock is mentioned once in the Old Testament, in Proverbs 30:31: "the strutting rooster." In the New Testament, Mark 13:35 mentions "cockcrow" as the signal for morning. The only other reference is to the cock that crowed when Peter denied Jesus.

Hens

Jesus used a tender image in describing God's concern for wayward Jerusalem: "How often would I have gathered your children together as a hen gathers her brood under her wings...." (Matthew 23:37). Otherwise, chickens are mentioned only perhaps in the provisions for Solomon's table ("fatted fowl" in 1 Kings 4:23) and at Nehemiah's table ("fowls...were prepared for me" in Nehemiah 5:18). They were not native to Palestine.

Partridges

The partridge is mentioned only twice, once in a reference to hunting it in the mountains (1 Samuel 26:20), and once in Jeremiah 17:11, where it "gathers a brood which she did not hatch." The Hebrew word for partridge is *qore* ("one who calls"), referring to the distinctive sound it makes. Three species of partridge are known in Palestine, where it is the most common gamebird.

Quail

Quail are mentioned in connection with only one event in the Bible. When the Israelites were in the wilderness, God sent quail into the camp in the evening and the people collected them for food. Quail are small gamebirds that migrate, but they can only do so with the help of the wind. The Bible states that they did come in on the wind (Numbers 11:31).

Cranes

The crane is a beautiful, large wading bird, with long neck, legs, and bill, similar to a heron. It is mentioned twice in the Bible. Isaiah 38:14 mentions its noisy call and Jeremiah 8:7 mentions its regular migrating habits.

Vultures

Hebrew and Greek each have only one word for vultures and eagles, since they are both large birds that fly high in the sky and are indistinguishable to the common person's eye. Both were (and are) common in Palestine. Proverbs 30:17 mentions being eaten by vultures and several other passages mention vultures circling overhead (Lamentations 4:19 and Matthew 24:28).

Fowlers

Fowlers were people who hunted wild birds, which were very common in Bible lands. Fowlers supplied birds for use as caged pets, for food, and as sacrifices. They most commonly caught birds using nets and snares, but they also used decoy birds, bows and arrows, slings, and throw-sticks. The references to fowlers in the Old Testament are metaphorical, usually speaking of their snares.

A golden eagle

Eagles

Eagles are mentioned more often than any bird of prey in the Bible. They are impressive for their great size, strength, speed, and soaring abilities. They are usually mentioned in stirring words: "You have seen...how I [God] bore you on eagles' wings and brought you to myself" (Exodus 19:4). "They who wait for the Lord shall renew their strength, they shall mount up with wings like eagles...." (Isaiah 40:31).

Storks

Storks are large, beautiful birds, standing more than three feet tall. They were considered unclean, however (Leviticus 11:19), no doubt because they feed in muddy places and eat mostly mice, frogs, fish, and small birds. They too are migratory birds, as Jeremiah 8:7 indicates.

Bats

Bats are mentioned at the end of the list of unclean birds (not to be eaten) in Leviticus 11. Isaiah 2:20 mentions men abandoning the idols they had made for themselves to the moles and the bats—to creatures living in dark and deserted places.

Foxes

Foxes were well known in biblical lands. Jesus mentioned the dens in which they sleep (Matthew 8:20), and their fondness for grapes is mentioned in the Song of Solomon 2:15. Judges 15:4,5 mentions Samson catching 300 foxes, tying them together with lighted torches between their tails, and sending them into the Philistines' fields. However, many scholars believe these were actually jackals, which are easier to catch.

Wolves

Wolves are large, predatory members of the dog family known for their ferocity. The imagery of wolves falling upon helpless flocks is very prevalent in the Bible. Jesus warned of false prophets who "come to you in sheep's clothing but inwardly are ravenous wolves" (Matthew 7:15).

Dragons

Dragons are found in both the Old and New
Testaments. In the Old Testament, the term is
sometimes more accurately translated as serpent, but
often it refers to the great monster of mythology. It
is a symbol of evil. In Revelation 12, it is a symbol
of Satan. Dragons are known from the literature and
art of the ancient Near East as well.

Wild Boars and Pigs

Hebrew had only one word for domesticated pigs
and wild boars. Both were on the lists of prohibited
foods listed in Leviticus 11 and Deuteronomy 14.
Psalm 80:13 refers clearly to the wild boar: "the
boar from the forest ravages [Israel]." The New
Testament speaks of swine several times, always in
pejorative references.

Satyrs?

Satyrs in classical mythology were forest gods, half
man and half goat. The Revised Standard Version
translates the Hebrew term *shair* as "satyrs" several
times, while the New Revised Standard Version
renders it "goat-demons" (Isaiah 13:21 and 34:14).
The references probably refer to a pagan deity with
the form of a goat that lured the Israelites to
worship it (Leviticus 17:7). Usually the Hebrew
term means "hairy one" or "male goat."

Lions

Hebrew has some nine different words for lions,
which suggests that lions were relatively common in
Old Testament times. Most Old Testament

references to them are figurative, referring to strength, but several historical incidents record lion attacks. In three cases in the Bible, lions killed people, and in each case, this was a punishment for them.

Paul and the Lion's Mouth

The Apostle Paul stated once that he was "rescued from the lion's mouth" (2 Timothy 4:17). Some see this as a reference to a lion in a Roman amphitheater. However, it comes in a context where Paul is speaking of opposition to him, and so others see a reference to the devil here. This is perhaps more likely, since the devil is spoken of as "a roaring lion, seeking someone to devour" (1 Peter 5:8).

Lions in the Ancient Near East

Lions were a favorite of kings. The Persian king kept lions in captivity during Daniel's day. In Egypt, lions were trained to help in the hunt; Ramses II was said to have kept a tame lion that went with him into battle. The Assyrian kings liked to hunt lions. In Roman times, lions were used in sporting events in which they fought each other, bears, and gladiators. Christians also were ordered thrown to the lions by some emperors.

The Lions' Den

The lions' den was a pit or trench in which lions were kept. It is mentioned in the story of Daniel, who was thrown there when he refused to stop praying toward Jerusalem (Daniel 6:16–24). When he was vindicated, his false accusers and their

Daniel in the lions' den

families were themselves thrown in the den and
devoured by the lions. This was not known
otherwise in the ancient Near East, but Job 38:39,40
does speak of lions crouching in their dens.

Deer

Several different words for deer are found in the
Bible. The "hart" is probably the roe deer. The
male of the species weighs up to 300 pounds and
has six-pronged antlers. It is not well suited for
desert living, which is reflected in Psalm 42:1: "As
the hart pants for streams of water...." The Bible
usually mentions deer metaphorically, referring
often to their graceful running and leaping abilities.

Gazelles

The gazelle is a type of antelope whose horns differ
from those of the deer. The gazelle has horns that

are hollow and do not branch. They are mentioned in the Bible for their speed and their beauty, and Isaiah 13:14 mentions the frightened "hunted gazelle."

Horses

Horses were common in biblical lands. They are mentioned more than 140 times in Scripture. In Old Testament times, horses were held by royalty, and they were a symbol of royalty and human power. In Israel, kings were not to accumulate horses, but to leave military matters to God. David kept a few horses after one battle, but his son Absalom was able to capture them during his revolt against his father.

Stalls and Stables

Several passages mention stalls, which were the compartments animals were kept in within stables. King Solomon had 4,000 stalls for horses and chariots (2 Chronicles 9:25). Archaeological remains of impressive stables and stalls have been recovered from Megiddo and other cities, dating to later periods in Israel's monarchy.

The War-Horse

Most references to horses in the Bible are to war-horses, listed as property of one nation or another. Job 39:19–25 has a magnificent description of the war-horse, speaking of its strong neck, its leaping ability, its majestic snorting, its fearlessness, and its zest for combat. Other passages speak of its speed and sure-footedness.

The fourth horseman, called Death

The Four Horsemen of the Apocalypse

Revelation 6 mentions four magnificent horses and their riders, representing the evils to come at the end of the world. The first horse was white, representing conquest; the second, red, representing war; the third, black, representing famine. The fourth horse was pale, its rider's name was Death. It represented war, famine, pestilence, and wild beasts, all at once.

Elephants

Elephants are not mentioned directly in the Bible, although ivory (from elephants' tusks) is frequently mentioned. During the time just after the Old Testament, elephants were used in the military. The famous Black Obelisk of Shalmaneser III, an Assyrian king from about 858 to 824 B.C., shows Assyrian vassals bringing elephants and monkeys to Shalmaneser as tribute.

Bears

Bears are rare in today's biblical lands, but the Syrian brown bear was more common in biblical times. They are mentioned several times as fierce animals, but only twice are bears referred to in actual historical episodes. The first story is when David killed both bears and lions that threatened his sheep (1 Samuel 17:34–37). The second story is about two bears that came out of the woods and killed 42 boys who were tormenting the prophet Elijah (2 Kings 2:23,24).

Monkeys

Monkeys are only mentioned in a list of goods that King Solomon imported from overseas: "Once every three years the fleet of ships of Tarshish used to come bringing gold, silver, ivory, apes, and peacocks" (1 Kings 10:22). They were not native to Palestine.

Five Golden Mice

When the Philistines captured the Ark of the Covenant, God struck them with a plague that was manifested by the outbreak of tumors (1 Samuel 5). It was probably transmitted by mice (or rats). In response, the Philistines made five golden mice and five golden tumors and sent them into Israelite territory with the Ark, hoping to stop the plague.

Sacred Trees

Sacred trees, called asherahs, were a part of almost every ancient Near Eastern culture. These were part of the sites of many sacred cults. In the Bible, these trees were forbidden to the Israelites. Some of these trees may have represented the Canaanite goddess Asherah, a consort of the god Baal.

Cedars of Lebanon

King Solomon used wood from the stately cedars of Lebanon in making his Temple. These trees can grow to a height of 120 feet, with a circumference of up to 40 feet. The wood is fragrant, free of knots, and is not attacked by insects. Once very plentiful in Lebanon, cedars are now very rare there. They are the country's national emblem today, appearing on its national flag.

The Tree of Life

The Tree of Life is one of two special trees mentioned in Genesis 2. God placed it in the Garden of Eden as a symbol of eternal life. After they sinned, Adam and Eve were no longer allowed access to it. The Book of Revelation speaks of

Adam and Eve

people eating of its 12 fruits and being healed by its leaves in the new creation.

The Judas Tree

This is the name given to a tree that Judas supposedly hung himself from (Matthew 27:5). It has reddish flowers that look like drops of blood. The flowers appear before the leaves, and the flowers spring straight out of the trunk itself, as well as from the new wood on the branches. The tree is the *Cercis siliquastrum*. Tradition states that the tree weeps blood each spring in memory of Judas.

Sycamore Trees

The prophet Amos was a "dresser of sycamore trees" by profession (Amos 7:14). The figs of the sycamore tree require cutting open with a knife point at a certain stage to help in the ripening process, and Amos did this. Branches of the sycamore tree are strong and wide-spreading, and Zacchaeus climbed such a tree in order to see Jesus better (Luke 19:4).

Willow Trees

The willow tree is mentioned several times in the Bible. The true willow was a small shrub or tree growing near water, and it flourished in the Jordan Valley. Psalm 137:2 mentions that the Jewish exiles in Babylon hung their harps on the willows there, but this tree was probably a variety of the aspen or poplar tree, such as the tall Euphrates aspen.

Almond Trees

Joseph's father, Jacob, gave Joseph's brothers a present of rare delicacies that included almonds to take to their brother (Genesis 43:11). The tree's blooming in late January is a sign that spring is coming. Almonds served as models for the cups of the golden lampstand in the Tabernacle.

A Rod of Almond

A striking word-play on the word for almond is found in Jeremiah 1:11. God showed Jeremiah an "almond" rod (*shoqed*), to illustrate the point that God was "watching over" (*shaqad*) his own Word to perform it.

Aaron's rod turns into a snake.

Aaron's Rod

Moses' brother Aaron, the high priest, had a very interesting rod. On one occasion, it turned into a snake that devoured the Egyptian magicians' rods/snakes (Exodus 7:12). On another occasion, it sprouted buds, blossoms, and almonds overnight; this was in a contest with the rebellious people concerning priestly authority (Numbers 17:8). This rod was kept in the Ark of the Covenant (Hebrews 9:4).

Date Palms

The Bible mentions many fruits, including apples, figs, dates, pomegranates, grapes, nuts, and olives. The date palm was one of the most valuable fruit trees in biblical lands. Almost every part of the tree was used: the fruit, pits, leaves, trunk, crown, and the branches.

Lilies

The Bible mentions lilies many times, but the term probably refers to different plants in different cases. Carved lilies (probably water lilies) were part of the Temple's decorations. The lilies of the field were probably the poppy anemone, the white daisy, or the crown marguerite.

Thistles and Thorns

More than 20 words in the Bible describe thistles, thorns, brambles, and other prickly plants. They are mainly mentioned symbolically, when talking about fruitlessness or worthlessness. Abimelech, a ruthless pretender to the throne in early Israel, is compared to the lowly bramble. Jesus told a parable of thorns choking off seeds, comparing this to the snuffing out of faith in some new believers' lives.

Herbs and Spices

The Bible mentions about 15 to 20 herbs and spices, not all of which can be precisely identified. Some—such as cinnamon, aromatic cane, stacte, galbanum, and frankincense—were used to make sweet-smelling incense for religious purposes. Others—such as mint, dill, cumin, onions, and garlic—were used in preparing food. Still others—such as cassia, aloes, and spikenard—were used for cosmetics and medicines.

The Olive Branch

The olive branch has become an international symbol of peace and good will. This imagery comes from its association with the dove and the story of

Noah, where a dove released from the ark returned with an olive branch in its beak (Genesis 8:11).

The Rose of Sharon

The Song of Solomon compares a man's lover to the "rose of Sharon." It was not a rose as we know it today, but probably a tulip of some kind, either the *Tulipa montana* or the *Tulipa sharonensis*.

Sweet Cane

Isaiah 43:24 mentions sweet cane. A wild cane is found throughout Palestine, but most scholars think this refers to the sugar cane. Honey was the most important sweetener in Old Testament times, but this cane was probably chewed or used to sweeten drinks and food.

Hemlock and Wormwood

The King James Version mentions hemlock twice, but modern versions translate the word in question as "poisonous weed" or "wormwood." Wormwood is mentioned several times in the Old and New Testaments—it was known for its bitter, unpleasant taste. It came to symbolize sorrow, tragedy, and even cruelty.

C. S. Lewis's Wormwood

In C. S. Lewis's fictional book *The Screwtape Letters,* about the correspondence between two devils, one devil is named Wormwood. His job is to poison the mind of the human being assigned to him. This imagery is taken from Revelation 8:8–11 where a star named Wormwood fell from heaven and poisoned the waters on earth.

The Temple

The Temple in Jerusalem was a magnificent building. Solomon had it built in about 960 B.C., but it was completely destroyed by the Babylonians in 586 B.C. The Persians allowed the Jews to rebuild it in 516 B.C. Around the time of Jesus, many additions were made to it by King Herod and others, but it was destroyed by the Romans a short time later, in A.D. 70. Today, the Islamic Dome of the Rock stands were the Temple once stood.

Dome of the Rock and the Western Wall

The Tabernacle: Precursor to the Temple

God gave Israel detailed instructions for building a portable tent—the Tabernacle—to house the Ark of the Covenant and other sacred items before Israel settled down in the promised land and built a Temple. The Tabernacle was richly appointed with expensive fabrics, and many of its features were recalled in the later Temple. The Levites erected and dismantled the tabernacle whenever Israel traveled.

Solomon's Temple

Solomon's Temple was a dazzling attraction. It was built using materials collected by his father, David. These included tons of stone blocks; boards of cedar, olive, cypress, and algum trees; metals including gold, silver, bronze, and iron; fabrics of purple, violet, and crimson; and beautiful arrays of alabaster, antimony, onyx, and all kinds of colored and precious stones.

A Perfect Cube

The Temple was carefully planned, including the details of its dimensions. It was an impressive structure, some 90 feet long, 45 feet wide, and 3 stories high. The innermost room, the Holy of Holies (or Most Holy Place), was where the Ark of the Covenant resided, symbolizing God's very presence. The Ark's dimensions formed a perfect cube, 20 cubits (about 30 feet) on each side.

The Ark of the Covenant

The Ark was Israel's most holy object. It was an ornate box made of acacia wood, overlaid with

gold, and topped with a golden mercy seat flanked
by two winged cherubs. It served as God's throne or
footstool on earth, and it contained the tablets of
the Ten Commandments, a pot of manna, and
Aaron's rod. It was kept in the Most Holy Place of
the Tabernacle and the Temple, but it was destroyed
by the Babylonians in 586 B.C.

No Cupids Here

Cherubim, or cherubs, were winged creatures
found in the Tabernacle and Temple. Two small
cherubim flanked the mercy seat of the Ark, two
large ones flanked the Ark itself in the Temple, and
cherubim were also woven into the fabric of the
Tabernacle and its great veil. Many artistic
representations of cherubs survive from the ancient
Near East, usually having some animallike features,
such as the body of a lion.

The Seven-Branched Lampstand

The Tabernacle and the Temple had a seven-
branched lampstand (menorah) for light. A picture of
it appears on the Arch of Titus, in Rome, as it was
being carried away after the Temple's destruction in
a.d. 70. The Talmud prohibited the making of any
seven-branched menorahs outside the Temple.

A Quiet Construction Site

The Temple site was so holy that the raw building
materials, including the huge stone blocks for the
foundations and the walls, were prepared away from
the site, and then brought to be installed in place.
No tools—hammers, axes, or any iron tools—were

heard on location, so that even the sounds of construction could not desecrate the site.

Gold, Gold, Gold

Much gold was used in Solomon's Temple. The interior faces of the stone walls were covered with fine wood, and then overlaid with gold. We are told that the weight of gold coming in annually during Solomon's reign was 666 talents, or almost 50,000 pounds (1 Kings 10:14). In today's dollars, that would be worth almost $2.5 billion. Indeed, gold was so plentiful during Solomon's reign that silver was considered almost worthless.

Bronze Pillars With Funny Names

The Temple had two tall, freestanding, bronze pillars at its entrance. Both had decorated bowls (possibly fire bowls) on top. The pillars stood more than 30 feet high, and both had names: *Jachin,* meaning "(God) will establish," and *Boaz,* meaning "in him is strength." When the Babylonians destroyed the Temple, they took these away with them for the valuable metal.

A Messy Affair

Worship at the Temple was often messy business, since it involved the killing and cutting up of so many sacrificial animals, including bulls, oxen, goats, sheep, and birds. When Solomon dedicated the Temple, 22,000 oxen and 120,000 sheep were sacrificed according to 1 Kings 8:63. Sacrificial altars had special channels on the sides for carrying away all the blood.

Misuse and Abuse of the Temple

Judah's kings often neglected the Temple, and it fell into disuse and disrepair. In Nehemiah's day, he found that his nemesis Tobiah actually set up private living quarters in one of the Temple's storerooms. In the intertestamental period, a Greek ruler entered Jerusalem and set up an altar to the god Zeus in the Temple courts. Jesus found people buying and selling all manner of things in the Temple courts in his day.

Destructions of the Temple

The Babylonians destroyed Solomon's Temple in 586 B.C., but it was rebuilt by the Jews 70 years later. In 20 B.C., Herod the Great launched an 80–year rebuilding program. In A.D. 70, the Romans destroyed this Temple, and it has never been rebuilt. The Arch of Titus in Rome depicts the sacking and looting of the Temple.

The Second Temple

The Temple that Jesus knew was first built in 516 B.C., but it was greatly expanded by King Herod and his successors into a magnificent structure with many impressive courtyards, chambers, colonnades, and gates around it. The finished product took more than 80 years to complete. Jesus had forseen that it would be destroyed.

An Impressive Engineering Feat

King Herod was a prolific builder. His greatest project in Jerusalem involved the Temple and its supporting platform. The Temple hill was sloped on

Model of Herod's Temple

all sides, so Herod had large terraces constructed, made of huge limestone blocks and filled with rubble, to enlarge the platform. The Temple Mount measured roughly 984 feet by 1,640 feet (300 meters by 500 meters), and in some places the height of the walls reached a little over 164 feet (50 meters)!

No Gentiles Allowed

Only Jews were allowed to pass beyond the outer courtyard of the Temple, the Court of the Gentiles. Warning signs in Greek and Latin were posted at regular intervals forbidding others to enter, on pain of death. The Book of Acts records a near riot

when Jews thought that the Apostle Paul had taken
one of his Greek friends into the inner courtyards.
Two such notices, engraved on limestone blocks,
have been found.

The Wailing Wall

The Western Wall of the Temple Mount is a section
of the retaining wall of King Herod's great Temple
complex. It is a place of prayer, where Jews through
the centuries have expressed their grief over the
Temple's destruction, the long exile, and their hope
for a return to their homeland. Because so much
lamentation and weeping took place at this wall, it
became known by non-Jews as the Wailing Wall.
Today, Israelis generally call it the Western Wall.

The Place of the Trumpeting

A priest would blow a ram's-horn trumpet (the
shofar) to announce the beginning of each week's
Sabbath, according to several Jewish sources.
Recent excavations have uncovered a limestone
block on the cornerstone of an ancient tower on
the southwest corner of Herod's great Temple
Mount that announces that it was "for the place of
the trumpeting."

The Pinnacle of the Temple

During the tempting of Jesus, the devil told Jesus to
throw himself off the pinnacle of the Temple to
prove that God's angels would save him. This was
probably the southeast corner of the great Temple
Mount, where the walls dropped into the Kidron
Valley, about 15 stories below.

Jesus and the Temple

Jesus freely came and went in the Temple and its courtyards. Under the colonnades of the outer court, the Jewish scribes and Pharisees taught the Law and held their debates. It was here that the 12-year-old Jesus impressed these rabbis with his knowledge. It was also here that an angry Jesus overturned the tables of the moneychangers and the merchants because they had turned God's house into "a den of thieves."

Illegitimate Temples

The Temple that Solomon built in Jerusalem was to be the one true sanctuary for Israel's worship. However, another Israelite temple was built at Arad in the Negev Desert during the time that Solomon's Temple stood. Jews at Elephantine, an island colony on the Upper Nile, also erected a temple in the fifth century B.C. This temple incorporated worship of many gods, not just the biblical Yahweh.

A Priestly Scepter?

A beautiful small ivory pomegranate with a Hebrew inscription on it surfaced in Jerusalem in 1979, dating to the eighth century B.C. The inscription connected it with the Jerusalem Temple and the priests. It was probably the head of a small scepter, or else an ornamental decoration in the Temple.

The Synagogue

The synagogue was the place of public prayer and worship that arose when the Temple was destroyed in the sixth century B.C. No sacrifices were carried out here; rather, reading of the Scriptures replaced this as the central event of Jewish worship. Over time, each Jewish community had its own synagogue. By medieval times, the synagogue had developed into the educational, civic, and cultural, as well as religious center of the community.

Synagogues and the Temple

Synagogues existed even while the Temple stood. A dedicatory inscription for a synagogue was found in 1902 near Alexandria, Egypt, dating to the third century B.C. Another dedication stone was found in Jerusalem in 1913; this is beautifully preserved, dating to the time of King Herod (37 to 4 B.C.). It was written in Greek, and tells of the synagogue's builders, its purpose, and some of its facilities.

How Quickly Can I Go?

No human institution has had a longer continuous history than the synagogue, and few have had a greater impact. It was—and remains—the central place of Jewish life. The Talmud praised synagogue worship in glowing terms, including this statement: "When a man leaves the synagogue, he should not march with hasty steps; but when he goes to the synagogue, it is right to run."

The "Ark" of Sacred Scrolls

An ark is not just a boat! A synagogue "ark" is a kind of cabinet or closet that holds copies of the Torah (the Law of Moses) and is the focal point of synagogue architecture. The Torah scrolls are large, beautifully ornamented, and painstakingly copied, with colorful and ornate calligraphy in the margins. They are kept in a curtained alcove, and only brought out by the rabbi for public reading. In Orthodox synagogues, the ark is placed against the wall nearest Jerusalem.

Which Way Do I Pray?

In Jewish custom, one prays facing Jerusalem, a tradition that goes back as far as Daniel, who prayed three times a day toward Jerusalem (Daniel 6:10). Later, when most Jews lived west of Jerusalem, a decorated plate or plaque was hung on the eastern wall of synagogues and homes to indicate the proper orientation for prayer. The plate or plaque, and even the synagogue wall itself, was called the *mizrach* (literally "east").

The Highest Building in Town

According to postbiblical Jewish law, the synagogue should be built on the highest point in a town; any building higher than the synagogue was to be destroyed. As a result, many synagogues in the Middle Ages had a pole on the roof, in order to comply technically with this rule.

Synagogue Mosaics

Synagogues have always been beautifully constructed. Many early synagogues had spectacular mosaics laid out on the floor, some covering the entire synagogue compound. These were intricately done, with thousands of small stones, and even their brilliant colors have been preserved.

A mikveh in Jerusalem

A Religious Bath?

Since the periods between the Testaments, Jews have used a ritual bath, or *mikveh,* to "bathe" converts to the Jewish faith. This ceremony cleanses away the former life. The mikveh was also used for ritual washings of Jews who had become ritually unclean. The Christian rite of baptism may have had its roots in this practice.

Syrian Artwork in the Synagogue

Impressive artwork decorated the walls of many ancient synagogues. A stunning discovery was made in the 1930s of a synagogue at Dura–Europus in eastern Syria, which was completed in A.D. 255.

Half of its walls were still standing, and they were decorated with many beautiful paintings of biblical scenes, including Abraham offering Isaac, Moses and the burning bush, and David playing his harp.

How to Build a Synagogue Service

Ten adult males are required to be present for a public service to proceed. This service consists of five parts:

(1) Reading of the Shema
(2) Synagogue Prayers
(3) Reading from the Torah (the Law of Moses)
(4) Reading from the Prophets
(5) Benediction

The Shema

The Shema is the classic statement of Israel's monotheism and God's providence, taken from Deuteronomy 6:4–9 and 11:13–21; and Numbers 15:37–41. Its name is derived from its first word, *shema*, "hear," and its first sentence has been the foundation of Judaism throughout the centuries: "Hear, O Israel, the Lord is our God, the Lord is one (or 'the Lord alone')." It was an important part of both morning and evening services in the synagogue.

Early Christians, Churches, and the Synagogue

Today's Christian worship service owes its origins to the synagogue service, because the earliest Christians considered themselves still to be Jews. Jesus himself attended and taught in the synagogue (Luke 4:16–21). The apostles Peter and John went

Christ teaches in the synagogue.

to the Temple to pray (Acts 3:1), and the Apostle Paul regularly went to synagogues first when he arrived in a city.

The Seat of Authority

In the synagogue, the rabbi normally is seated on a small platform when he teaches. The reading of the Bible was done standing, out of respect for the Scriptures. Visiting rabbis were allowed to read the Scripture portions and teach, which Jesus did on occasion.

181

Pentecost: Early Harvest Feast

This feast was so named because it comes 50 days after the first sabbath of Passover—*pent* means 50. It is also known as the Feast of Weeks, First Fruits, or Harvest. It was a spring festival celebrating the completion of the grain harvest. Acts 2 tells us that Christians received the Holy Spirit on the day of Pentecost and spoke in languages not their own. Today, Pentecostals are Christians who practice speaking in tongues.

"The Pentecost" by El Greco

Biblical Festivals

The Mosaic Law established seven festivals. Three of these were great pilgrimage festivals that were related to the agricultural calendar: the feasts of Passover, Pentecost, and Tabernacles. The two high holy days—the Day of Atonement and New Year's Day—and two days of rest—the weekly Sabbath and the monthly New Moon festival—completed the festivals. The festivals of Purim and Hanukkah arose later.

The Day of Atonement: Erasing Sin

This was an annual day in the fall for fasting and rest (not feasting), and atoning for the nation's sins. This included careful cleansing of the high priest, the Tabernacle itself, and the people. Many offerings were sacrificed. It remains a high holy day for Jews today and is called Yom Kippur.

Passover: Festival of Remembrance

Passover, or the Feast of Unleavened Bread, was a spring festival associated with the barley harvest. It commemorated the Israelites' flight from Egypt, when God's angel of death passed over and spared the Israelites (but not the Egyptians), and when the Israelites fled so quickly that they had no time to let their bread rise.

Feast of Tabernacles: Fall Harvest Festival

This was also known as the Feast of Ingathering or Booths, and it was the greatest of the festivals. For seven days, the Israelites lived in booths or temporary shelters made out of branches and the harvest's fruit, to remind them of their desert accommodations and God's protection when they left Egypt. Even today, many Jews still erect ceremonial *sukkahs* (booths) in their backyards.

The Feast of Trumpets: New Year's Day?

A solemn day of rest, memorials, and sacrifices was set aside on the new moon of the seventh month and trumpets were blown on this day. In postbiblical times, it came to be associated with the New Year, the *Rosh Hashanah,* celebrated in the fall.

The New Moon Festival: A Monthly "Sabbath"

A monthly festival of rest, special sacrifices, and blowing of trumpets was observed at the new moon. The prophet Amos denounced greedy merchants who could not wait until the New Moon Festival was over so they could get back to their dishonest business practices. The new moon of the seventh month was set aside as a special day, known as the Feast of Trumpets.

Hanukkah: Festival of Dedication

The festival of *Hanukkah* (or "Dedication" mentioned in John 10:22) celebrates the rededication of the Temple in 164 B.C. after its desecration by Greeks. The festival, also called the Festival of Lights, lasts for eight days. According to the Talmud, the Jews found a lamp in the Temple with a one-day supply of oil, but it stayed miraculously lit for eight days of celebration. Today, the festival serves as an occasion for remembering and thanksgiving.

The Jubilee Year

The jubilee year was to come after seven sabbatical years, or every fiftieth year (Leviticus 25). It was a sabbatical year for the land (thus allowing two fallow years), and also a year when all lands would revert to their original owners. Also, anyone who had sold himself into service (because of debts) would regain his freedom. The idea was noble, but there is no record that either the sabbatical or jubilee years were ever actually observed.

Purim: Reversal of Anti-Semitism

Purim is the joyful festival in the Book of Esther, ordered by Mordechai to celebrate the Jews' great reversal of fortune. The Jews had been under an edict of death, but not only did they escape death, but they were also able to kill their enemies. The events show an early example of the many tragic, state-sponsored persecutions that have been directed against Jews.

The Sabbath: Day of Rest

The seventh day of the week was a day of rest, because God had rested from creating the world on the seventh day. The Jewish Talmud identified 39 main categories of work that were to be avoided on the Sabbath and devoted one lengthy part to spelling out how the Sabbath was to be observed and not profaned. Still today, Sabbath celebration begins at sundown on Friday evening, when Jewish families gather for a special meal. On Saturday morning, they go to the synagogue, and the rest of the day is spent resting, eating, and reading the

Jesus and the disciples at the Last Supper

Bible. The Hasidim liked this day so much they called it "Princess Sabbath."

Signs From the Liver

In many biblical lands, priests and prophets practiced divination of omens by examining animal entrails and the markings of their livers. The liver was so important for this that detailed clay models were made, with various lobes and lines marked and sometimes even inscribed with omens and magical formulas.

Sabbath Breaking

The Sabbath day was very important. Not only could people rest and be refreshed, but they were reminded of God's great creation (Exodus 20:11). If people defiantly disobeyed God and worked on this day, the penalty was death (Exodus 31:15 and 35:2). Once, a man found gathering wood on the Sabbath was stoned to death (Numbers 15:32–36).

The Sabbatical Year: A Humanitarian Policy

The Law provided for the land to lie unplanted every seventh year (Exodus 23 and Leviticus 25). This corresponded to the pattern of a weekly Sabbath and it allowed the land needed time to rest. More importantly, whatever grew in the fields was to be left for the poor and marginal members of society. Also, debts were to be canceled in the seventh year, allowing people a fresh start.

Sunday: The Christian Sabbath?

Most Christians celebrate Sunday as a day of rest. This is to remind them of Jesus' resurrection from the dead on that day. For many Christians, this choice of day is also a conscious rejection of what they regard as Old Testament ritual law, which Christians are no longer subject to. Other Christians do celebrate the Sabbath on Saturday, to remind them of the Old Testament Sabbath day.

Prophets and Crystal Balls

Prophets were men and women sent by God to speak for him to the people. Contrary to a popular

The prophet Isaiah

stereotype, their major role was not to be crystal-ball gazers, predicting the future for curiosity seekers. Rather, they were sent to address contemporary situations. They often had very harsh words to say to kings and the people, and, as a result, they were usually not very popular.

Lilith, the Queen of Demons

This creature is mentioned only once in the Bible, in Isaiah 34:14; she is included among the creatures of deserted places. In rabbinic literature, she is an evil night creature with wings and long flowing hair. According to legend, she was Adam's first wife, but she was sent away because she demanded full equality with him. She took her revenge by trying to kill all newborn babies.

Never Bite the Hand That Feeds You

Many kings liked to have their own prophets to give them advice. These court prophets usually told the king only what he wanted to hear. The most famous were the 450 prophets of Baal that Ahab kept, and another 400 who claimed to be prophets of God (1 Kings 18,22). A few court prophets, such as Nathan and Gad, did confront the kings with true words from God.

Jeremiah and Hananiah: Prophetic Showdown

A dramatic confrontation between a true and a false prophet was between Jeremiah and Hananiah (Jeremiah 28). Hananiah claimed to speak for God and he offered a soothing message to the people, while Jeremiah's message was much harsher—he prophesied war, famine, and pestilence. Jeremiah was vindicated when he correctly foretold Hananiah's imminent death.

What? No Tea Leaves?

Just as many people today read tea leaves or their horoscopes for signs and omens, so too the ancients tried to read about their futures. They observed animal and human behavior for signs, and they also observed such things as oil drops on water, patterns

of rising smoke from incense burners, and movements and the interrelationships of planets and stars.

Dreams

Interpretation of dreams was an important means of discerning the will of God in biblical times. Every ancient king retained court wise men to interpret dreams. Joseph and Daniel are the best-known dream interpreters in the Bible. Daniel was even required to tell the Babylonian king what the king had dreamed, and then interpret it for him.

Ecstatic Frenzies

The Bible mentions some prophets practicing a form of prophecy in something like an ecstatic frenzy, accompanied by noisy musical instruments (see especially 1 Samuel 10:5–13). This phenomenon was well known throughout the ancient Near East. One ancient Mesopotamian text speaks of the ravings of a *mahhu* (this was the Assyro–Babylonian title for the ecstatic prophets) as follows: "I am smitten down like a *mahhu*. That which I do not know, I bring forth."

The Red Heifer

An important means of purification in Israel involved killing an unblemished red heifer, one that had never been yoked. It was burned outside the camp along with aromatic woods, and then the ashes were mixed with water. Anyone who had become ritually unclean could wash in this water and be purified. The red color probably was chosen as a reminder of blood.

Sympathetic Magic

Almost 4,000 years ago, the Egyptians made pottery bowls and figurines upon which they would write the names of their enemies (called Execration Texts). They would then smash these items to pieces, hoping that this would induce their gods to crush these enemies for them. One bowl mentions some pre-Israelite rulers of Jerusalem.

The Evil Eye

The Hebrew term for evil eye in the Old Testament means "a miserly, grudging, or envious look." However, outside the Bible, it reflects a widespread ancient belief that an envious or hostile glance by someone with special powers could cause harm. This belief is found in postbiblical Judaism as well.

Laws of Cleanness and Uncleanness

The Israelite ceremonial law went to great lengths to distinguish between the realms of the clean and the unclean, and to prescribe rituals of cleansing. Sources of uncleanness included unclean animals, bodily emissions, various skin diseases (especially leprosy), and corpses. The basic purpose was to remind the Israelites of the great gap between them and God. The people needed to prepare themselves to meet with God, and they needed to do so properly and reverently.

Clean and Unclean Animals

Unclean animals were determined by several criteria. The two most important were hygiene and pagan practices. Unhygienic animals were scavengers and birds of prey, since they feed on rotting flesh. Pigs and scaleless fish were also unclean. Animals used in pagan worship or in witchcraft were unclean, such as pigs, fish, dogs, mice, hare, and various insects. Animals that were not typical of their class were also unclean.

What Was a Nazirite?

Nazirites were people—man, woman, or slave— who took special, voluntary vows "to separate themselves to the Lord" (Numbers 6:2). The vow included not drinking wine, not cutting one's hair, and not going near a dead body. Samson, Samuel, and John the Baptist were life-long Nazirites, dedicated by their parents (although Samson violated all of the vows). The Apostle Paul took a short-term Nazirite vow.

Samson slays a lion.

Blood

Blood represented life in the Bible, and shed blood represented death. The sacrifice for sin required the shedding of blood. This was true whether the victim was an innocent animal or the ultimate sacrificial lamb, Jesus. Because of its special significance, Jews were to drain blood from meat before eating it. This is required for a kosher diet.

The Avenger of Blood

In many ancient societies, the relative of someone who was killed had the right to take vengeance for the death. Cain feared for his life because of this when he killed Abel. The Law of Moses accommodated this practice, but carefully regulated it. The Law distinguishes between accidental and deliberate homicide, provides cities of refuge, and requires the approval of the council of elders with two testifying witnesses before vengeance can be taken.

The Body and Blood of Christ

Christians celebrate the sacrificial death of Christ by eating and drinking bread and wine. The broken bread symbolizes Christ's broken body and the wine symbolizes his shed blood. Some Christians believe that these elements actually become the body and blood of Christ when a priest blesses them during the ceremony of the Eucharist (or mass).

The Holy Grail

This was the cup supposedly used by Jesus at the Last Supper with his disciples. It became the subject of many legends in the Middle Ages. At King Arthur's Round Table, an empty seat was reserved for the knight who found the Grail. In the early twentieth century, an ancient silver cup (known as the Chalice of Antioch) was publicized as being the Holy Grail, but it is usually dated no earlier than the fourth century A.D.

Palm Sunday

In Christian tradition, the Sunday before Easter has come to be known as Palm Sunday. This was because people welcomed Jesus into Jerusalem by spreading leafy branches on the road before his donkey as he was entering the city at the time of Passover (in the spring). The cutting of palm branches was usually practiced in the fall, at the Festival of Tabernacles, as part of the construction of the booths (Leviticus 23:40–42).

Palm Branch Waving

The four types of branches that are mentioned in Leviticus 23:40, which includes palm branches, were to be held in one's hands during the reciting of the Hallel (Psalms 113–118), according to later Jewish custom. The palm branches were to be shaken three times in each direction of the four corners of the earth, symbolizing the abundance that comes from God in heaven.

Pilate's Hand Washing

The Roman governor Pilate washed his hands at Jesus' arraignment to symbolize his withdrawal from responsibility for whatever might happen to Jesus (Matthew 27:24). This practice was not new to him; undoubtedly it was a widespread custom. The Old Testament has many examples of ritual hand washing to symbolize innocence (Psalm 26:6 and Deuteronomy 21:6–8).

Hand Washing in Judaism

Ritual cleansing of the entire body was important in the Old Testament, but in Judaism the practice of ritual hand washing attained prominence. Jews washed their hands before and after meals, along with saying a prayer of blessing. They also washed their hands on other occasions, too, such as when getting out of bed or before offering daily prayers. This naturally resulted in good hygienic habits.

Foot Washing

Since people wore open sandals and traveled dusty roads in Bible lands, their feet had to be washed frequently. This is mentioned several times in the Old Testament (see Genesis 18:4). Not washing one's feet was a sign of mourning (2 Samuel 19:24). It was considered to be the work of a menial slave, but Jesus washed his disciples' feet in order to emphasize the necessity of serving others (John 13). The practice persists today in some Christian groups as a rite of worship.

Christ is helped with his cross by Simon, a Cyrenian.

A Cross to Bear

The expression "That's a cross I have to bear" comes from Jesus' words in Matthew 16:24: "If any want to become my followers, let them deny themselves and take up their cross and follow me." Prisoners condemned to death by crucifixion often were forced to carry their own crossbeam—it was a sign of impending death. Today, the phrase denotes a resignation to carrying a heavy (usually emotional or psychological) load.

How Long Was Jesus Dead?

The total time Jesus was dead was not much more than 36 hours. According to the Gospels, Jesus died on a Friday afternoon, about 3:00 p.m. He was placed in a tomb that evening and remained there until some time early Sunday morning, before the women got there. The popular notion of three days comes from the Jewish way of counting days, in which any portion of a day counts as a full day.

Music in the Ancient Near East

Almost every one of Israel's neighbors had rituals to worship their gods, and music played an important part, just as it did in Israel. Archaeologists have uncovered many pictures of musical instruments, as well as several tablets that explain ancient musical scales.

A Joyful Noise

Worship in the Temple was a noisy event. Cymbals, castanets, rattles, and tambourines were played along with harps, lyres, trumpets, and wind instruments. Men played only certain cymbals and women played particular tambourines, and over time these instruments became closely associated with either men or women.

Singing and Dancing

Singing and dancing were essential components of the worship of God. The Israelites celebrated military victories with excited singing and dancing, and often women led the way. David danced a joyful and frenzied dance when the Ark entered Jerusalem. Great choirs led singing in the Temple courts.

The Ram's Horn

The eerie sound of the ram's horn trumpet announced the great religious festivals in ancient Israel. The *shofar,* which is the Hebrew word for this horn, still calls Jews to worship in the synagogue on the eve of the New Year (*Rosh Hashanah*) and the Day of Atonement (*Yom Kippur*).

The Priests: Primary Religious Authorities

The priests were the main religious leaders in Israel. They offered the sacrifices for people's sins. While they could not forgive people's sins, they were the "middlemen" between the people and God. They were experts on God's word, too. When people wanted to know an answer to a question about the Bible, they asked the priests (Haggai 2:11–13). The priests were supposed to be from the tribe of Levi and descendants of Aaron.

The High Priest

The high priest was the highest religious authority in Israel. His garments were very impressive (Exodus 28). On his chest was a breastplate with the names of all twelve tribes of Israel, symbolizing his

Priests (high priest in middle)

role as the people's representative before God. He was the only person who could enter the holiest place in the Tabernacle and the Temple. Moses' brother, Aaron, was the first high priest.

Barefoot Priests

The priests performed many, if not all, of their duties in the Tabernacle and Temple barefooted. This was because of the sacredness of the ground on which they walked. God told Moses to remove his shoes at the burning bush because he stood on holy ground as well.

A Dangerous Profession

The high priest was the only one allowed to enter the Holy of Holies in the Tabernacle and Temple. Because of the awesomeness of God's presence, and the potential danger of desecrating the holy place, the priest wore golden bells in order to be heard. If the bells went silent, everyone knew that something was wrong. Imagine if a priest fainted or died in the Holy of Holies. A custom even arose whereby a rope was attached to the high priest so he could be pulled out should he die!

The Tabernacle

The Tabernacle: God's Home in the Wilderness

The Tabernacle was a large portable tent that served as God's "home" when the Israelites were in the wilderness. In it was the Ark of the Covenant and other holy things. It was made of fine boards covered with layers of rich fabrics (Exodus 26). The Levites were responsible for putting it up and taking it down whenever Israel traveled.

What Was the Tent of Meeting?

In most cases, this was another term for the Tabernacle. Its name indicates that it was a place where people could meet God. But there was also a separate tent called the "tent of meeting" (Exodus 33:7). This was one that Moses used to pitch outside of the camp, where he and the people could also meet God. It was a temporary tent during the Israelites' days in the wilderness, and it was not known later in Israel's history.

Anath: A Bloodthirsty Goddess

Anath was the Canaanite goddess of love and war. She was Baal's sister and consort. In one Canaanite text describing her actions, she intervened fiercely in a dispute between her brother and Yamm, the god of the sea: "She seizes Mot…with a sword she cleaves him, with a sieve she scatters him, with fire she burns him, in the millstones she grinds him, in the field she sows him."

Sacred Places

Besides the Temple and the Tabernacle, there were certain other places where people could go to speak with priests. There was a temple of the Lord at Shiloh before Solomon's Temple was built (1 Samuel 1). People also met at different times at Shechem, Bethel, Mizpah, mounts Ebal and Gerizim, and many other places to worship God.

High Places: Places of False Worship

The high places were sites of pagan Canaanite worship that the Israelites often went to. The

Israelites also built new high places of their own.
The high places usually were on a hill, and they had
an altar for sacrifices. The Israelite and Judean kings
were continually condemned for tolerating or
encouraging worship at these. Even many of the
good kings "did right in the eyes of the Lord, but
[they] did not remove the high places." Archaeol-
ogy has revealed two rival Israelite temples, one at
Arad (in southern Judah) and one at Elephantine
(on the Nile River). In addition, a sanctuary was
built at Bethel (Amos 7).

Yahweh the Bull?

The Bible prohibited any pictorial representations
of God, but a valuable find in the middle 1970s in
the Sinai Desert was a depiction of God as a bull on
fragments of a storage jar. An inscription above his
head reads "I bless you by Yahweh of Samaria and
by his asherah." This is a dramatic example of the
religious borrowing that was common in Israel and
that the biblical prophets warned against.

Dagon: Baal's Father

Dagon was the principal Philistine god. He was the
god of the storms and the grain harvest, whose
temple Samson destroyed in his last acts of strength
(Judges 16). Dagon was widely worshiped in all lands
of the ancient Near East. In portions of the Baal
mythology from Ugarit, Dagon was Baal's father.

Yahweh and His Asherah

The picture of Yahweh as a bull also has an
Egyptian god standing next to him and a seated lyre

player, who probably represented his asherah (the Canaanite goddess linked to Baal). If so, then this is an even more dramatic example of religious borrowing, by which Yahweh was given a wife or consort by some Israelites.

Artemis' Sacred Stone

One of the Seven Wonders of the Ancient World was the Temple of Artemis (Diana) at Ephesus. Paul's preaching against idolatry at Ephesus threatened the lucrative trade in religious souvenirs, since people came from all around to see the temple and "the sacred stone that fell from the sky" (Acts 19:35). Perhaps this was a meteor that landed there.

The Horns of the Altar

The altar of burnt offering was to have four horns (like the pointed horns of an animal such as a bull), one on each corner. These functioned as the ultimate place of refuge or security, since we see two men in danger of their lives desperately clinging to them for protection (1 Kings 1–2). When the prophet Amos announced that even the horns of the altar at Bethel would be cut off, he was saying that there was no more escape for that wicked city.

The Luck of the Draw

Many important decisions in biblical times were made by drawing lots. The sacrificial goat on the Day of Atonement was chosen by lot, and the promised land was apportioned by lot. Achan was revealed by lot as the man responsible for Israel's

Ancient lots

defeat at Ai, and Saul was chosen Israel's first king by lot. In the New Testament, soldiers cast lots for Jesus' garments, and the disciple who replaced Judas Iscariot was selected by lot.

The Queen of Heaven

Some Jews of Jeremiah's day in Judah and in Egypt worshiped an astral goddess known as the "queen of heaven." They baked cakes for her and burned incense to her. This goddess was probably the Assyrian and Babylonian fertility goddess Ishtar (the Canaanite Astarte, associated with the planet Venus), or the Canaanite goddess Anath (who is called "the queen of heaven, the mistress of the gods" in an Egyptian text).

Marduk: Babylonian High God

In the Law Code of Hammurabi, the god Marduk is accorded the highest status among the gods, taking over from Enlil. He retained this position until after the time of Christ. He was appealed to by an endless succession of Babylonian and Assyrian kings over the centuries. Jeremiah mentions Merodach's (Marduk's) shame (along with other idols) in a prophecy predicting the downfall of Babylon (Jeremiah 50:2).

Bronze Calf at Ashkelon

In 1990, a small bronze calf with traces of silver overleaf was found at Ashkelon, dating before 1550 B.C. It was less than four inches long and four inches high, and it was housed in a small cylindrical clay shrine with a small doorway. It served as an object of worship for the Canaanites who lived at Ashkelon, and it recalls the incident at Mount Sinai where the Israelites made a golden calf out of all their gold. Early press reports mistakenly called this figurine a golden calf.

Baal: Canaanite High God

Baal was the god of the storms (and fertility), bringing rain and productivity to the land. He was the highest of the Canaanite gods. His cult posed a greater threat to true worship in Israel than did any other cult, since the Israelites lived in closest contact with the Canaanites. King Ahab of Israel gave the first official sanction to the worship of Baal, an action that the prophet Elijah vigorously denounced.

Elijah and the Prophets of Baal

The prophet Elijah had a dramatic confrontation with 400 prophets of Baal, the Canaanite deity, on Mount Carmel following a long drought. Elijah was able to call down fire from heaven, following which it began to rain. Baal's reputation was severely damaged because he had not brought fire or changed the weather, despite his prophets' desperate pleas.

Canaanites and Child Sacrifice

Child sacrifice was a ritual practiced by some Canaanites, and by the biblical kings Ahaz and Manasseh. Evidence of the most systematic forms of child sacrifice comes from Carthage, in North Africa, where the Canaanite Phoenicians migrated. A sacrificial precinct there flourished for almost 600 years, with tens of thousands of children sacrificed.

Osiris: Chief Egyptian God

Osiris was the chief Egyptian god during biblical times. He was the god of the dead, of the netherworld, and the afterlife. His importance was that he offered the possibility of continued life, modeled on the life people had known. He became associated with the Nile, whose annual rise brought new life to the earth. His cult probably came the closest to a universal religion in Egypt in pre-Christian times.

Zeus: The Greek High God

Zeus was the sky god, lord of thunder, and giver of weather, enthroned on Mount Olympus. An altar to Zeus was erected in the Temple by foreign occupiers of Jerusalem in 167 B.C., which was a great desecration. Some scholars see the reference in Daniel 9:27 of a "desolating sacrilege" as a prediction of this event.

The New Covenant

The New Testament speaks often about the new covenant that God made with his people. Even the term "New Testament" means new covenant. The Old Testament mentions the new covenant by name only once, in Jeremiah 31:31: "Behold, the days are coming, says the Lord, when I will make a new covenant with the house of Israel and the house of Judah." Many other Old Testament passages speak of this covenant in indirect terms.

Ra: Egyptian Sun God

Ra was the sun god of Egypt, depicted as a man with a falcon head, wearing a sun disk. The dead could sail over the heavens by day in his sacred boat. Nearly every pharaoh for 2,500 years took the title "Son of Ra." The god is known in the Bible only in the name of Joseph's father-in-law, Potiphera, the priest of On (Genesis 41:45).

Ishtar: The Mother Goddess

Ishtar was a Canaanite and Philistine goddess mentioned many times in the Old Testament (as "Ashtoreth"; plural: "Ashtaroth"). She was known in Babylonia and Ebla as the goddess of love and war, and in Egypt as the goddess of war. She was also known at Ugarit as a consort of Baal (though his primary consort was Anath). The Greek form of her name was Astarte. Her cult of sexuality was a constant lure and snare to the Israelites.

The Athenians' Unknown God

When Paul was in Athens, he tried to establish a point of reference with his pagan audience by telling them that he had seen one of their altars dedicated "To an unknown god" (Acts 17:23). He then proceeded to tell them that the God he was preaching about was this unknown god. Later extrabiblical references, including a partially broken inscription, confirm the existence of altars of unknown gods at Athens.

Paul preaches in Athens.

Rachel's Household Gods

When Rachel left her father's household after she married Jacob, she took with her the family's household gods and hid them under her saddle. Her father, Laban, was alarmed enough to come after her and retrieve them. These were small idols kept in private households and consulted to get directions about the future.

The Dead Sea Scrolls

Thousands of biblical documents and fragments (dating two or three centuries before Christ's death) were discovered in 11 caves high up in the cliffs near the Qumran Brook, at the northwest corner of the Dead Sea, between 1947 and 1956. The first discovery was made by a Bedouin shepherd searching for lost animals. Many of the documents are biblical and many are nonbiblical (such as commentaries and devotional literature).

Circumcision: Not Just a Jewish Practice

Circumcision was an important rite in the Bible, symbolizing obedience to the covenant that God had made with his people. However, the Hebrews were not the only ancient people who practiced this. Edomites, Moabites, Ammonites, and even Egyptians also practiced it, at least to some degree. The Philistines were conspicuous for being uncircumcised (Judges 14:3).

The Qumran Community

The ruins of a community were found near the Qumran caves, where the Jews who produced the

Dead Sea Scrolls lived. They formed an ascetic community of priests and laypeople pursing a life of strict dedication to God, and they had a strong expectation that the Messiah would soon come. A scroll fragment made public in 1991 suggests that they may have been a branch of the dominant party of the Pharisees.

Star Gazing

Some Israelites engaged in worship of gods associated with the stars and the planets. Amos denounced this practice: "You also carried along Sikkuth your king and Kiyyun, your images, the star of your gods" (5:26). Sikkuth (or Sakkuth) was probably the Babylonian god Sak-Kut, or Ninurta, associated with Saturn, and Kiyyun (or Kaiwan) was probably Kayawanu (or Kainanu), the name for the planet Saturn.

The Dead Sea Scrolls and the Bible

The value of the Dead Sea Scrolls for the Bible is immense. Every Old Testament book except Esther is represented, and these represent the oldest actual copies of biblical texts in existence. The nonbiblical texts give us a first-hand picture of the thinking of one sect in Judaism during the time of the New Testament. This can provide much light on backgrounds of the New Testament.

Gnosticism Discovered

In 1945, peasants at Nag Hammadi, on the Nile River in Egypt, discovered 13 ancient books written in Coptic that were from a Gnostic community living there about A.D. 200. The Gnostics were condemned as heretics by early church leaders, and many pseudo-Christian beliefs are indeed represented in these texts, which include such tractates as the "Gospel of Thomas," the "Wisdom of Jesus Christ," and the "Apocalypse of Adam," along with portions of Plato's *Republic*.

The Seven Deadly Sins

This is the term used in the Middle Ages to refer to the seven sins thought to lead to damnation. They are pride, covetousness (greed), lust, anger, gluttony, envy, and sloth (laziness).

Paul addresses the people.

Christian Head Coverings

Christian tradition was the opposite of Jewish tradition, following the Greek custom: Men's heads were not to be covered during worship

(1 Corinthians 11:4). Indeed, this was a sign of dishonor to God. Women, however, were to have their heads covered as a sign of honor (11:5,6). Scholars disagree whether Paul meant that a woman's head covering was to be a veil or shawl, or merely long hair.

"My word is my honor!"

The importance of a spoken oath is indicated in a parallel from ancient Nuzi. In one court document, a spoken will is being contested in court. However, the court upholds the validity of the will, even though it was not written down. This is especially remarkable since it is found in a society in which written records have been found by the thousands!

The Ruler of the Synagogue

This was an official who presided over the board of elders, who had oversight for the functioning of the synagogue. Five individuals are mentioned in the New Testament as "rulers of the synagogue." Sometimes the entire board of elders was considered to be the "rulers," as when Paul and Barnabas received permission to preach from the rulers of the synagogue at Antioch (Acts 13:15). Their authority included the power to discipline and even to excommunicate people.

The Great Synagogue

The Mishnah (A.D. 200) mentions a "Great Assembly" (*Knesset ha-Gedolah*) of 120 men that was supposedly established by Ezra. It was the supreme legislative body for the Jews. Its origins and nature are murky, and it is not mentioned in the Bible (although Ezra's leadership in a great assembly of the people is described in Nehemiah 8–10). Today, the Israeli parliament (the Knesset) is named after this, and it also has 120 members.

The Sanhedrin

The Sanhedrin is much better known than the "Great Synagogue" as the supreme Jewish law council. It is mentioned several times in the New Testament, usually referring to Jesus' trial (where it is called the council). The Sanhedrin consisted of 70 members, plus a head (the high priest), and Jewish tradition traces its origins back to the council of 70 elders that Moses appointed in the wilderness (Numbers 11:16).

What! No Tattoos?

Leviticus 19:28 prohibits self-mutilation of any sort: "You shall not make any cuttings in your flesh on account of the dead or tattoo any marks upon you." This prohibition was mainly because such self-mutilation was practiced in several pagan cultures. A good illustration of this comes from the prophets of Baal who cut themselves with knives while they were trying to get Baal to send fire down from heaven (1 Kings 18:28).

Family Worship

Fathers were responsible for their whole households in religious matters, including servants. Fathers were the ones who would bring the sacrifices to the priests. Joshua spoke for everyone in his household when he said that he and his house would serve the Lord (Joshua 24:15). Entire families also made pilgrimages to Jerusalem to celebrate festivals (Luke 2:41–43).

Times For Prayer

In biblical times, people prayed at any time of the day or night. There were formal prayers for

Jesus prays in the Garden of Gethsemane.

morning and evening services in the Temple. Daniel prayed three times a day in his bedroom. Nehemiah prayed while he was working: Several times he uttered quick, impromptu prayers under his breath when a crisis arose. Jesus also prayed often—from early morning to late at night.

Too Much Praying?

While prayer was to be practiced at any time, even unceasingly (1 Thessalonians 5:17 says "pray constantly"), it was to be done reverently and meaningfully. Jesus warned about idly and endlessly repeating empty phrases in prayer (Matthew 6:7). One Jewish rabbi went to the extreme of stating that Jews should not pray every hour of the day, so that they would not get into the habit of calling on God mindlessly, thus leading to disrespect.

Draft Deferments

The Law provided for certain people to escape military service under certain circumstances (Deuteronomy 20). These included those who had built a house and not yet dedicated it, and those who had planted a vineyard and not yet enjoyed its fruits. The principle behind this was mostly humanitarian, but it also illustrates the importance of personal property, and the inheritance rights that go along with it.

A Year-Long Honeymoon

Military exemptions applied to anyone who was engaged to be married (Deuteronomy 20:7). Furthermore, newlywed men were to be exempted

from military service or any other business for a full
year. This allowed for a good start to the marriage
(Deuteronomy 24:5). These humanitarian concerns
show an important feature of the Law, which was
essentially for people's good.

The Judges: Israel's Deliverers

The judges were charismatic military leaders God
had raised up to deliver Israel from its enemies. The
judges included Deborah, Gideon, Jephthah, and
Samson. They only lived during a short period in
Israel's history, before the kings. Some of the judges
also judged Israel in a judicial sense, such as
Deborah and the "minor" judges. However, this
judicial activity was not as important as their
military activity.

The Kings as Religious Leaders

The priests were the primary religious authorities in
Israel, but the kings also had religious duties. They
were supposed to be examples for the people. They
were to read and obey the Law and lead people in
doing the same (Deuteronomy 17).

Water Baptism

Baptism with water was an integral part of the early
Christians' lives. Jesus himself was baptized. Peter
preached, "Repent, and be baptized...for the
forgiveness of your sins" (Acts 2:38). Jewish custom
stressed ritual washings, but baptism was really a
Christian development. Most early baptisms were
by water immersion, but pouring and sprinkling
developed as alternate modes.

Satan tempts Jesus.

Going the Extra Mile

In the Sermon on the Mount, Jesus spoke repeatedly about going beyond the minimal requirements of law or social courtesy in order to show true generosity of spirit. One vivid illustration was when he said "if any one forces you to go one mile, go with him two miles" (Matthew 5:41). This referred to a detested Roman practice of forcing civilians into the service of carrying military baggage for a prescribed distance, which was one Roman mile.

The Temptation of Christ

The Book of Hebrews states that Jesus, even though he was God, was tempted to sin just as we are but he was able to resist the temptation (4:15). This is part of an argument that he identifies with our struggles. The Bible says nothing about the normal temptations he probably faced growing up, but it does record the three temptations by Satan at the beginning of his public ministry (Matthew 4).

The Baptism of the Holy Spirit

Several times Jesus prophesied about a baptism that would be from the Holy Spirit after he had left the earth. John the Baptist stated that his baptism was with water, but Jesus' was different: "he will baptize you with the Holy Spirit and with fire" (Matthew 3:11). Paul spoke of all believers being "baptized into one body" by one Spirit (1 Corinthians 12:13). This means that Christians would be filled and covered with the Spirit as they were covered by water in baptism.

Paul and Adoption

Adoption was common in Greek and Roman cultures. Under Roman law, the adoptee left his old status and entered into a new relationship as a son to his new father. His old debts were canceled and he started a new life. He had all the rights and responsibilities of any natural-born children. Paul used this beautiful imagery to portray what happens to believers: They are adopted into God's family as his own children (Romans 8).

Jewish Head Coverings

Jewish males traditionally have worn a skull cap for prayer and meals. This was regarded in the Talmud as a sign of reverence for God. Indeed, the Talmud indicates that rabbis did not walk even four steps with their heads uncovered. This custom may have arisen from the priests' head covering mentioned in Exodus 28:37–39.

"Let your yea be yea"

This expression comes from Jesus' words in the Sermon on the Mount, when he stated that people should not swear falsely, nor should they take any oaths by heaven or by Jerusalem or by anything else. A simple yes or no should be binding. The King James Version says, "let your communication be, Yea, yea; Nay, nay" (Matthew 5:37).

"My word is as good as gold!"

Most people know that Esau sold his birthright to his brother Jacob for a bowl of stew. Jacob then tricked his father into pronouncing the blessing on

Isaac blesses Jacob.

him. When the trick was discovered, Isaac was unable to revoke it. Isaac was bound to his oath, and so he could only pronounce a very vague, generic blessing on Esau.

The Worm and the Toothache

One of the best-known incantations used in ancient Babylonia is one intended to rid the sufferer of a toothache. It tells of how the worm had asked Shamash, the sun god, where he could dwell. He asked to be allowed to dwell in the gums of people and live off their blood. The text then curses the worm for this. The sufferer was to repeat the curse three times, in hope of relieving the pain.

Rabbinic Keys

In rabbinic literature, giving keys symbolized the granting of authority. Rabbi Akiva stated that God would give the angels Michael and Gabriel the keys to open the 40,000 gates to hell. Another Jewish belief held that God held four keys in his hand: the keys to rain, conception, resuscitation of the dead, and crops.

The Key of David

Eliakim was made the grand vizier, or steward, over the household of King Hezekiah (Isaiah 22:15–25). He was given "the key of the house of David" to wear on his shoulder. This symbolized his exclusive authority to grant access to the king. This image is picked up in Revelation 3:7, where Christ now has "the key of David," and he alone opens the door of access to God.

Peter's Keys

Jesus told Peter that "I will give you the keys of the kingdom of heaven, and whatever you bind on earth shall be bound in heaven" (Matthew 16:19). This was a statement of the authority he received. The Roman Catholic tradition has held that this authority was exclusively Peter's, and, through him, the Church's. Protestant traditions have held that Peter represents the apostles, and the authority refers to the wider apostolic message and mission.

King Hezekiah's storehouse

Who Were the Levites?

The Levites assisted the priests in doing their work, but they could not offer sacrifices themselves. They also took care of the Tabernacle and (later) the Temple. They took the Tabernacle down and set it up whenever the Israelites traveled. They formed one of the twelve tribes, but they did not receive any separate land, except for 48 "Levitical cities" scattered throughout the other tribes' territories.

Everyday Life in Israel

For most people, life was hard. Men and women worked hard in the fields raising crops or animals, and whole families helped out during harvest or sheep-shearing time. Houses were small and cramped, and many people slept in the same room. Beds were usually straw mats on the floor. The women also worked hard preparing and cooking food, and managing their households.

Farmers harvesting dates.

Recreation

Even though life was hard for most people, they still found time for games. Many of their games were related to military practices, such as running, wrestling, and shooting slingshots or bows and arrows. Paul used athletic word pictures, often comparing the Christian life to running a race.

Children's Games

Many children's toys have been found in Israelite towns. These include whistles, rattles, marbles, dolls, and toy animals. Israelite children also kept pets, such as birds. Children danced, sang, and played games in the streets when they were not working. In 2 Kings 2, a band of small boys amused themselves by making fun of Elisha the prophet.

Cave Dwellings

There are many caves in Palestine, and early in history people lived in them. But the Old Testament does not mention anyone living in caves except in emergencies. Lot and his two daughters lived in a cave after Sodom and Gomorrah were destroyed. David and Elijah both hid in caves when their lives were in danger. The prophet Obadiah hid 100 prophets of the Lord from the wicked queen Jezebel in two caves.

For Sale: Roomy Tent, 2BR, No Leaks

The Hebrew patriarchs lived in large tents that were probably very much like the tents that Arab nomadic sheepherders live in today. These tents are made of goat's-hair fabric, which keeps out the rain and the heat. There are three seven-foot-high tent-poles in a row down the middle, and two rows on the outside. This design creates two rooms, one for women and children and one for men and where guests are entertained.

The Israelite Four-Room House

During the time of the monarchy in Israel, the most common type of house had four rooms. One room was long, running along the back wall. The other three rooms were side-by-side, next to the long room. People would enter the house through the middle room. Usually this room was used as a courtyard. This was a typically Israelite design, distinguishing Israelite settlements from Canaanite ones.

Building Materials

Almost all Israelite houses during Old Testament times were made of mud bricks. Sometimes rough stones were used along with the mud bricks. The walls were coated with waterproof plaster on the inside. The floors were made of hard-packed clay. Wealthier homes had floors paved with smooth stones. The roofs were made from wooden beams covered with branches, which were then filled in with mud plaster to make a flat surface.

The World's First Clothes

Before Adam and Eve sinned, they did not wear any clothes and they were not embarrassed. After they sinned, they were ashamed and made clothes for themselves. Their first clothes were not very

Adam and Eve being sent out of the Garden of Eden.

substantial, however. They made aprons for themselves out of fig leaves. Later, God made them better clothes out of animal skins, which symbolized the animal sacrifices that would have to be offered for sin.

Men's Dress

Most men wore a loincloth around their waists and a shirt or robe under their outer clothes. Their outer clothing included a colored garment, covered by an outer cloak or mantle. Men wrapped this around themselves for warmth and slept in it at night. They took it off for work and sometimes carried things in it. They also wore cloth turbans or headpieces as protection against the sun.

Women's Dress

Women's clothing was similar to men's, but it was made of finer materials, had more colors, and women wore veils. They too had robes they wore under their outer garments. Their outer garments and headgear also protected them from the sun. Rich women wore a long train or veil.

Did They Wear Kilts, Too?

Daniel 3:7 mentions the bagpipe along with many other musical instruments that were played when people fell down and worshiped Nebuchadnezzar's golden statue. This bagpipe would have been made of goatskin, with two pipes protruding.

Priests' Garments

Priests' clothing was very colorful and expensive (Exodus 28). Ordinary priests wore a cloth covering their hips and thighs and a long linen tunic with sleeves. They also wore beautiful belts made of blue, purple, and scarlet cloth and a kind of a turban. The high priest wore a very expensive breastplate made of gold and expensive linens. The breastplate had twelve precious stones on it—one for each tribe of Israel.

Shoes and Sandals

Sandals were the simplest and most common type of shoes that people wore. They were usually made of woven reeds or several layers of leather. Many shoes had uppers, too, which provided more protection against the cold in the winter and against stones, briers, and hot sand in the summer.

Army Boots?

Soldiers had to have much sturdier shoes than
ordinary people, since they marched long distances
over very rough ground. They also needed more
protection for their legs and feet. They wore high-
topped leather shoes that reached up and laced to
the knee. Greek and Roman soldiers wore nail studs
in their shoes.

Precious Stones

About 30 different types of precious stones are
mentioned in the Bible. These include many-
colored agates, reddish-purple amethysts, green
emeralds, red garnets, clear diamonds, green jade,
yellow-brown jasper, blue lapis lazuli, green
malachite, white onyx, pale opals, shiny pearls, red
rubies, blue sapphires, many-colored topaz, and
blue-green turquoise. Many of these have been
discovered set into beautiful settings of gold and
silver.

The World's Earliest Schools

The oldest known schools were in ancient Sumer,
dating to about 2500 B.C. These were scribal
schools, where students copied texts over and over
on clay tablets to practice their writing. This
practice also helped them learn many subjects in the
process. They studied botany, zoology, geology,
geography, mathematics, languages, and other
studies. Only the wealthy could afford the scribal
schools, however, so literacy was limited mainly to
the rich. It was not until the time of Jesus that
schools became open to nearly everyone.

Nurses in Israel

The midwife was the Israelite equivalent of a visiting nurse or public health worker. The Hebrews had professional midwives when they lived in Egypt who refused to obey the pharaoh's orders to kill Hebrew baby boys (Exodus 1). A midwife also helped Tamar when she had trouble giving birth to twins (Genesis 38).

Ancient Jewelry

Jewelry is mentioned often in the Bible, and much has been found in excavation in all Bible lands. Early in history, it was made of bone chips, shells, and colored stones. Later, precious stones and metals were used more often. Many gold and silver necklaces, bracelets, earrings, and rings and beautiful precious stones have been found.

Belts and Sashes

Loose belts were used mainly to keep people's robes from blowing around too much, since they did not wear pants. But sometimes a belt was used to hold a sword. Belts were made of leather or cloth and were often folded and wrapped around the waist.

Synagogue Schools

Sometime during the period between the Old and New Testaments, formal Jewish schools for children were started in the synagogues. By the time of Jesus, all Jewish children had to go to school. They learned how to read and write by studying the Bible. It is possible that Jesus himself went to such a school, where he learned the Torah.

Medical Doctors in the Bible

Joseph used doctors to embalm his father, Jacob, in Egypt (Genesis 50:2). In Israel itself, King Asa of Judah sought medical help from doctors when he was sick (2 Chronicles 16:12). Usually God was the one who healed people in Old Testament times. Luke, the author of the books of Luke and Acts, was a medical doctor. By the New Testament time period, medical science had advanced remarkably.

What Is Threshing?

After a crop was harvested, it had to be *threshed,* which means beating the grain with sticks or grinding it under big stones or heavy threshing sledges. This was so the kernels of grain could be separated from the straw. The prophet Amos made effective use of the threshing image when he condemned Damascus for "threshing" Gilead "with threshing sledges of iron" (Amos 1:3).

Worry About Crops and Harvest

Life in Bible times was tightly bound up with the cycle of the seasons and the availability of food. Most of the Canaanite high gods were associated with the natural forces that brought rain and sunshine, since people lived only one bad year away from starvation. Joseph made a name for himself when he warned the pharaoh about an impending seven-year famine. Joseph organized food storage and distribution programs to combat the famine (Genesis 41). Joseph was reunited with his family because they had to go to Egypt to get food during the famine.

A Palestinian farmer turns over the soil in his olive orchard.

Planting and Harvesting Seasons

A very important calendar for the crop year was found in the biblical city of Gezer. This crop year begins in mid–September. It mentions two months of the olive harvest, two months of planting grain, two months of late planting, a month of hoeing flax, a month of barley harvest, another month of harvesting the other crops, two months of grape harvesting, and a month of summer harvest for harvesting the summer fruit.

Farming Villages

Farmers in Palestine lived in small, crowded villages not far from their fields. Usually these villages were clustered together within a few miles of a walled city. That way, people in the villages could be under the protection of the fortified city if attackers came, but they were still close enough to their fields to work them.

Crop Planting

Israelite farmers plowed their fields with a simple hand plow made of wood, with a cone-shaped metal tip. This tip fitted over a wooden tailpiece that went into the ground. Plows were usually pulled by a team of oxen or sometimes donkeys. The farmers planted seeds by scattering them on the fields by hand.

Harvest Time

Life in Bible lands depended upon the harvest. It had to be brought in quickly, so everyone in the family and all the servants helped. The workers would use curved wooden sickles with iron blades to cut the stalks of grain. They would hold a bunch of grain in one hand and cut it with the sickle in the other hand. Other workers would collect these small bundles and tie them into larger bundles, called sheaves.

What Is Winnowing?

Winnowing means throwing the entire mixture of threshed grain into the air so the wind could blow away the straw (or chaff). The heavier grains fell to the ground and were saved. The grain was then ready for storing or selling. Psalm 1 speaks of the insignificance of the wicked in God's sight as "chaff which the wind drives away."

Jesus turns water into wine.

Wine

Wine was the most common drink besides water in the ancient Near East. It is seen in the Bible as something positive, marking joyous celebrations and solemn religious occasions alike. Jesus' first recorded miracle was to turn water into wine.

Storage Silos

Grain was stored in storage silos and barns in the ancient world. The Bible mentions full storehouses as being a blessing of God and empty ones as God's curse. Joseph was in charge of the storehouses of Egypt when the famine came (Genesis 41). An impressive underground stone-lined silo has been excavated from Megiddo, which was one of Solomon's store cities (1 Kings 9:19).

Dove's Dung

The Revised Standard Version in 2 Kings 6:25 mentions "dove's dung" selling for a good price during a siege of Samaria. Other versions have "locust beans" (New English Bible) or "wild onions" (New American Bible). It was a bulb that was roasted or boiled before eating. Today, the plant is known as the star of Bethlehem.

The Staff of Life

The term "staff of life" refers to a dietary staple, such as bread, rice, or potatoes. Bread was the staff of life in the ancient Near East. The phrase probably comes from Leviticus 26:26, which mentions the "staff of bread." The word *bread* is often used for food in the Bible. This is why, in John 6:35, Jesus refers to himself as "the bread of life."

Boaz: A Generous Farmer

The Law of Moses had many humane provisions for the poor, widows, orphans, and the like. One stated that farmers should not harvest every last corner of

Ruth and Boaz

their fields or vineyards, nor should they go back
and pick up what had fallen during the reaping
process. These were to be left for the poor and
resident aliens to pick up (Leviticus 19:9,10). We
see Boaz putting this into practice in a heartwarming story in Ruth 2.

Breads

Most bread was made from barley or wheat, but
other grains were also used. The grain was ground
into flour by using a mortar and pestle or with
millstones, and then baked over a fire on heated
stones, a griddle, or an oven. Leaven (to make the
bread rise) was used to make round, flat loaves. The
unleavened bread was flat and thin, much like
today's pita bread.

Ovens

Clay ovens were used in all biblical lands for making bread. A fire was built on stones in the floor, and then the coals were raked out so that the bread dough could be placed against the hot inner walls to bake or on the hot stones themselves. Common fuels were wood, charcoal, dried grasses, and weeds.

Mint, Dill, and Cumin

These were green herbs mentioned by Jesus in his condemnation of many Pharisees' hypocrisy (Matthew 23:23). He said that they scrupulously gave a tenth of their supply of these herbs to God, in legalistic observance of the law, but that they neglected the more important things, such as justice, mercy, and faithfulness.

Harvesting the Fruit of the Vine

Grapes grew on vines in vineyards. Keepers of vineyards had to hoe the ground and trim the vines, taking off dead branches. The vines were trimmed (or pruned) with small knives with hooked blades. The grapes were then picked at harvest time.

Wine Making

Grapes were used primarily for making wine. They were dumped into shallow basins cut out of stone. The juice was squeezed out by people stepping on the grapes, after which the juice was placed into deep vats to ferment into wine. Grapes were also dried in the sun to make raisins. Sometimes the raisins were pressed together into raisin cakes.

Jesus is offered vinegar while on the cross.

Vinegar

Vinegar is acidified or sour wine. Bread dipped in
vinegar was used for refreshment by laborers in the
fields (Ruth 2:14), and Jesus was offered vinegar to
drink on the cross (Mark 15:36). Psalm 69:21
testifies to its vile taste: "they gave me poison for
food, and...vinegar to drink."

Solomon: No Vegetarian He

Meat was expensive food, served to guests only on very special occasions. Meat was common in royal palaces, however, because kings could afford it. The normal meat ration for one day in King Solomon's court was 10 oxen, 20 beef cows, 100 sheep, along with deer, gazelles, roebucks, and game birds (1 Kings 4:23)!

Fruits and Vegetables

Figs, dates, and pomegranates were the most common fruits eaten in Israel, after grapes, and they are mentioned frequently in the Bible. Apples, pears, apricots, quince, peaches, and melons are also known from the ancient Near East. Vegetables mentioned in the Bible include rice, lentils, beans, leeks, garlic, onions, and cucumbers.

Melons

The Israelites ate luscious watermelons and musk melons when they were slaves in Egypt. These have been cultivated there since earliest times, and were an inexpensive food for the captive Israelites. When they were in the parched wilderness, they longed for these juicy fruits and complained bitterly about their lack.

Honey

The product of honey bees was a valued luxury during much of the Old Testament period, although in the New Testament wild honey was food for outcast John the Baptist (Matthew 3:4). Most honey was wild, but people brought honey from domesticated bees on at least one occasion to the Temple, among the other first fruits of the harvest (2 Chronicles 31:5).

Spicy Foods

The Israelites spiced up their food with leeks, onions, and garlic when they lived in Egypt. They sorely missed these when they were eating nothing but manna and quail in the desert wilderness. Even today, many Israeli and Arab foods are flavored with exquisite spices.

"Salt that has lost its flavor"

This expression comes from Jesus, who compared his disciples to salt and their uselessness if they lost their "flavor," their commitment to Christ (Mark 9:50). Strictly speaking, sodium chloride (salt) is a stable compound and does not lose its saltiness. However, most salt in Palestine came from the Dead Sea, where other minerals and sand were mixed with it. The salt could dissolve, leaving a useless, tasteless compound.

Olive Farming

Olives grow on trees that are grown in olive orchards. These short, twisted trees do not need much attention until harvest time. In biblical times, olives were usually picked by hand, but sometimes they couldn't be reached so the farmers had to shake them off gently or beat the branches with long twigs or sticks. The olives then were crushed and pressed so the oil could be collected for its many uses.

The Israelites collect manna.

Manna

The Israelites were provided with "bread from heaven" in the wilderness. It appeared each morning as a fine, white, flaky substance on the ground that tasted like wafers and honey. Its name (Hebrew *man*) came from the puzzled Israelites, who asked "*man-hu?*" ("What is it?"). Certain insects in the Sinai Desert produce similar droppings, but not in such great quantities nor as often as told of in the Bible.

Olive Oil

Along with bread and grapes, olive oil was the third most basic food. It was mixed with flour to make bread and cakes, and these were often cooked in the oil. It was also used as a fuel for lamps, in religious ceremonies, and as a medicinal ointment.

Oil Lamps

Oil lamps were the common means of lighting in biblical homes. They were made of clay or iron, and they burned olive oil for fuel. Thousands of oil lamps have been found, from all periods. Early lamps were flat bowls, and then a spout began to evolve with a pinched edge at the rim.

The Job Market

The basic occupations during Biblical times were the ones related to food and shelter. Farmers and shepherds provided food for people to eat. Women prepared and cooked the food, and they made cloth out of animal hair, from which they made clothes and tents. Builders built houses and palaces for people to live in.

Humane Lending Laws

The Bible did not forbid lending or even taking interest, but it did regulate these practices carefully. Israelites were not to take interest from the poor (Exodus 22:25). If someone fell into debt, he could sell some property, or even himself into service, to repay the debt. However, the property had to be returned or he had to be released in the jubilee year (Leviticus 25).

Lending Laws Respecting Human Dignity

If someone made a loan and a cloak or something else was put up as collateral, the lender was to respect the borrower's dignity by not entering his house to seize the collateral. He had to wait outside for the borrower to bring it out. If the borrower was poor, the lender also had to return the cloak each night, since that was what the borrower slept in (Deuteronomy 24:10–13).

Biblical Merchants

Many different types of merchants produced products for sale, which were often sold at the city gate. In larger cities, tradespeople of the same trade lived in the same neighborhood. So there would be the potters' section of town, the food market, the cheesemakers' valley, and so on. Nehemiah mentions the "Tower of the Ovens," which suggests bakeries clustered together (Nehemiah 3:11).

"I'm off to war! See you soon!"

Ancient Near Eastern kings usually launched their military campaigns in the spring after the rainy season had ended. In Assyria, kings went out on a new campaign every year or two. Even the Bible mentions such a custom: "In the spring of the year, the time when kings go forth to battle ...." (2 Samuel 11:1).

The Trades

Carpenters and woodworkers made homes, tools for farming, and weapons for war. Many workers worked in quarries and mines, digging for stone, salt, iron, copper, gold, silver, and other minerals. Many people became metalworkers, shaping tools, weapons, and jewelry. Potters also were very important. Indeed, broken pottery is one of the most common things found in ancient towns during archaeological excavations.

Samson and Delilah

Biblical Barbers

The Bible records several actual incidents of cutting hair. Samson's lover Delilah betrayed him by having a man cut off his hair while Samson slept. Job shaved his head when he mourned. An Ammonite king humiliated David's servants by shaving half their beards. Ezekiel was to shave his head and burn or scatter the hair, in a symbolic act. The Apostle Paul cut his hair after taking a Nazirite vow.

Fishing

Fish were a common food in Bible lands, and the Bible talks about many methods of catching them. Several different types of nets are mentioned. Fishhooks also are referred to in Isaiah 19:8: "the fisherman...cast a hook in the Nile." The spear and harpoon are referred to in Job 41:7.

Fishing Nets

The New Testament mentions different types of nets used in fishing. These include the small cast net that was thrown out by hand, and the large drag net that was several hundred yards long and whose two ends were laboriously hauled into shore. Many of Jesus' disciples were fishermen, and the Bible also mentions the work of maintaining the nets, including washing (Luke 5:2), spreading and drying (Ezekiel 47:10), and mending (Matthew 4:21).

On Ships

The Israelites were not seafaring people, but ships and boats are mentioned many times in the Bible. Ships were vessels of commerce and of war in ancient times. The Egyptians painted many pictures of their trading ships and warships that crossed the Nile River and the Mediterranean Sea. Assyrian reliefs show many Phoenician ships and other

Biblical fishermen collect the fish from their nets.

vessels. In later times, Roman and Greek cultures were spread in large measure by ships.

The Galilee Boat

Jesus spent much of his time around the Sea of Galilee, and even on fishing boats in the sea. In 1985, such a boat from Jesus' time was recovered from the mud of the seabed, which was exposed during a drought. The boat would have been rowed by four men, could hold up to 15 men, and could easily have accommodated Jesus and his disciples.

What's a Talent?

The talents in Jesus' parable of the master who gave his servants several talents were units of money. These were enormous sums of money, since the Greek *talanton* weighed between 57 and 95 pounds, and one talent was more than 15 years wages for a laborer. The modern English meaning of talent as ability was derived by expanding the meaning of the Greek word in this parable.

Esther becomes queen after exposing Haman's evil.

Dangerous Times

The Bible records two acts directed specifically at all Jews by governments. In Esther, a decree was issued by the Persian king ordering the extermination of Jews, a decree that, fortunately, was not carried out

(Esther 3). Acts 18:2 tells of a decree by the Roman emperor Claudius that expelled all Jews from Rome.

There Are Arks and Then There Are Arks

Hebrew has two words that are translated as "ark" in English. The most common refers to the Ark of the Covenant. The rarer word refers to Noah's ark and is also used for the basket of bulrushes that the baby Moses was placed into, Moses' ark.

Chariots

In the King James Version, eight Hebrew words and two Greek words are translated as "chariot." Horse-drawn chariots are known from the second millennium onward in the ancient Near East, and their introduction from the southern steppes of Russia revolutionized warfare. They were also used in peacetime for hunting, processions, and ceremonial rites.

Chariots: Ancient Tanks

Chariots were the ancient equivalents of modern-day tanks. They were very light, fast, and easily maneuverable. Chariot crews consisted of two to four men: a driver and one or more warriors, such as archers, spear throwers, and shield bearers. Chariots functioned best in flat terrain, so chariots in Israel are mentioned more often than in Judah. There were more hills in Judah.

Solomon's Chariot Cities

Solomon had Israel's greatest chariot forces. He had 1,400 chariots and 12,000 horses, which he imported from Egypt and Kue in Asia Minor

(1 Kings 10:26–29). He established chariot cities where he could store his forces, at Hazor, Megiddo, and Gezer.

The Philistine Monopoly on Iron

During the Early Iron Age (from 1150 to 1000 B.C.), the Philistines were Israel's major enemy and they held a monopoly of iron in Palestine. In 1 Samuel 13:19–21, it states that there were no smiths in Israel. Whoever wanted to sharpen a plowshare or another tool had to go down to Philistine territory, since the Philistines did not want the Israelites to make weapons.

The First Cisterns

The first plastered cisterns, cut into the rock and capable of holding large quantities of water without seepage, appeared in Palestine about 1200 B.C., marking a major improvement over the old, porous cisterns. Most older cisterns were pear-shaped, with a narrow opening and a bulbous reservoir. Joseph and Jeremiah were both imprisoned in empty cisterns, although Jeremiah's was nearly full of muck (Genesis 37:24 and Jeremiah 38:6).

Stoning

Stoning was a form of ritual execution for certain prescribed crimes. These crimes included sacrificing a child to the god Molech, practicing witchcraft, blaspheming God's holy name, and leading people astray to worship other gods. Stoning was also a product of mob violence: Stephen was stoned and died (Acts 7:54-60).

Stephen is stoned.

Impalement

The gruesome practice of impaling prisoners of war and criminals on stakes was practiced in several ancient societies. The Assyrians did this to prisoners of war, and the Persians did this as a criminal punishment, according to the Greek historian Herodotus. Haman's gallows in Esther were possibly a stake on which a person was impaled, rather than a hanging gallows.

Technology Transfer

By the early tenth century B.C., the military and technological tide had shifted in Palestine and the Philistines were no longer dominant, since Samuel, Saul, and David had subdued the Philistines. It is interesting to note that archaeological evidence from this period confirms this point. Blacksmiths from northern Palestine were producing iron, while Philistine sites show no corresponding technological advances.

A Cubit

The cubit was the distance from the elbow to the tip of the middle finger of a grown man. It was the standard measure of length among the Hebrews. The standard cubit was approximately 17½ inches long, while the royal cubit was longer, about 20½ inches. God told Noah to build the ark 300 cubits long and 50 cubits wide.

A Shekel for Your Thoughts

The shekel was the basic unit of weight in the ancient Near East. It was small, about four-tenths of an ounce. Small shekel weights in various denominations were used to weigh things on the scales. The shekel is the basic coin in Israel today.

Embalming

Embalming was not done in Israel; it was a distinctively Egyptian invention, and it was usually reserved for kings and persons of some repute. Two individuals are mentioned in the Bible as having been embalmed: Joseph, a Hebrew who had risen high in the Egyptian court, and his father, Jacob.

Solomon's Bath

No, we aren't talking about how clean he was. The Hebrew *bath* was a unit of liquid measure, equal to almost six gallons (the royal bath was twice that). But the Hebrew word is not related to the English word. The large bronze "sea" in front of Solomon's Temple had a capacity of 2,000 baths.

Ancient Baths

Washing and bathing were done in all biblical periods for religious and health reasons. Large public baths were introduced by the Greeks and Romans, and many remains of these have been found. Jesus healed a man by the Bethesda Pool, in the northeast corner of Jerusalem. This pool supposedly had healing properties.

Jesus heals the man by the Pool of Bethesda.

Ancient Hot Springs

Hot mineral springs were valued for their supposed healing properties. The Jewish historian Josephus mentions hot spring resorts at Tiberias in Galilee and at Callirhoe near the Dead Sea during the biblical period. A large Roman bath complex dating to the third century A.D. was excavated in the 1980s near the Sea of Galilee—it contained more than a dozen pools. These were fed by hot springs that still exist today.

Baths for Foreigners

An inscription found in a synagogue in Jerusalem dating before A.D. 70 mentions its "bathing establishment for those from abroad." This may refer to the Pool of Siloam (John 9:7), near which the synagogue was found.

Ancient Well Discovered

The Hebrew patriarchs Abraham and Jacob dug numerous wells to provide water for their flocks. A remarkable well was excavated in the 1980s at Arad, in the Negev Desert of southern Israel. It is more than 10 feet wide and is neatly lined by stones to a depth of 68 feet, at the water level. Water was carried from the well to a channel cut into rock that took water within the city walls.

The Megiddo Ivories

The most impressive collection of ivories found to date was discovered in the 1930s at biblical Megiddo, dating before 1200 B.C. There were almost 300 artifacts, including decorated combs, circular jewelry boxes, mirror handles, fly whisks and fan stocks, game boards and gaming pieces, and a sundial.

Commemorative Pillars

The Hebrews used large standing stone slabs to commemorate important events or covenants. Jacob used a stone for a pillow at Bethel, and then set it up as a memorial of his encounter with God and poured oil on it. The Canaanites erected standing stones for worship, but the Israelites were prohibited from using these. An impressive set of ten pillars still stands at a sacred Canaanite site at biblical Gezer.

The Israelites cross the Jordan River.

Teachable Moments

"What does this mean?" was the question that Israelite children often would ask their parents when they saw certain memorial symbols. Joshua set up 12 stones to commemorate the crossing of the Jordan River (Joshua 4). Children would ask about the commandments of the Law (Deuteronomy 6) and the Passover feast (Exodus 12). In Jewish homes today, children still ask this question at Passover.

A Tassel for Remembering

The Israelites were to make tassels for the corners of their outer garments and tie a blue thread to each tassel so they would remember God's commandments. Jewish men today wear special four-cornered prayer shawls with these tassels during morning prayers and the Day of Atonement services.

The Star of David

The six-pointed star of David, which has two inverted triangles, is a symbol for Judaism, and it appears on the Israeli flag. The star was quite common as artwork and was used for decorative and magical purposes in early times by both Jews and non-Jews, including Christians. In Hebrew, it is called the *magen David,* "the shield of David."

The Blessing

Jewish family life has always had a rich texture to it, and part of this involved the blessing of children by their parents. The Hebrew patriarchs Abraham, Isaac, and Jacob all blessed their sons, and this practice has continued to the present. A widely practiced custom today is the blessing of children at the Sabbath meal.

Teach Your Children Well

Woodstock-era baby boomers will recognize a line from a popular song by Crosby, Stills, and Nash, but the thought goes back much further than that. In Deuteronomy 6:7, the Israelites were instructed to teach God's commandments "diligently to your children, and shall talk of them when you sit in your house, and when you walk by the way, and when you lie down, and when you rise."

Paul preaches at Ephesus.

The Ephesus Theater

Acts 19 mentions a riot instigated by the Apostle Paul's presence at Ephesus, which spilled over into the great Roman theater there. This theater is typical of the countless fine Roman and Greek theaters built throughout Mediterranean lands. These theaters held large crowds but still had perfect sight lines for the audience, and were models of good acoustics.

Durable Roman Aqueducts

The Romans constructed magnificent aqueduct systems for cities throughout their empire. Jerusalem's aqueducts brought water into the city from as far away as 25 miles. These aqueducts were refurbished and used in many later periods, including under the British Mandate in 1918.

Crucifixion: Cruel and Unusual Punishment

Execution by crucifixion was normally reserved for the lower classes in Greek and Roman societies, usually slaves. It was a humiliating and excruciatingly slow, painful death. Prisoners were normally whipped until blood flowed, then they were either tied or nailed to the cross and left to die of gradual suffocation brought about by fatigue.

Hanging

Hanging in the Old Testament meant the public exposure of a body after death. This was done as a warning to others, but a body was not exposed overnight (Deuteronomy 21:22,23). Two suicides were apparently by hanging: Ahithophel's (2 Samuel 17:23) and Judas Iscariot's (Matthew 27:5).

Death

Death was the focus of much attention in almost every ancient Near Eastern society, where elaborate rituals and cults of the dead grew. The most elaborate systems arose in Egypt, where the pyramids and the great tombs of the kings were built to provide the pharaohs with everything necessary for the life to come. The Bible speaks of spiritual death differently; it is the eternal separation from God.

Dial-A-Mourner?

The prophet Jeremiah speaks of professional women mourners who could be summoned and who would "start a wailing for us." This skill was passed on to their daughters and even their neighbors (Jeremiah 9:17–20). But the Bible forbade any excessive displays of mourning for the dead: "you shall not cut yourselves or make any baldness on your foreheads for the dead" (Deuteronomy 14:1). These self-destructive customs were practiced by many of Israel's neighbors.

Grave Robbers Beware!

In 1878, a Greek inscription labeled as an "Ordinance of Caesar" was brought to Europe, probably from Nazareth. Many scholars date it to about A.D. 50. It was 20 lines long and it proclaimed capital punishment for anyone who violated a grave in any way. This was an unusual feature of Roman law at this time.

The angel tells the women that Jesus is risen.

Jesus' Tomb and the Nazareth Decree

If the Ordinance of Caesar (also known as the Nazareth Decree) dates to A.D. 50, then the emperor Claudius issued it some 20 years after Jesus' death and resurrection. Some Jews said that Jesus' body was stolen from the grave (Matthew 28:11–15), so Claudius' decree may have been in reaction to this story. If so, it is the first extrabiblical indication that the Roman government was aware of Jesus.

Care for the Dead

Dead bodies were well cared for in all ancient societies. In the New Testament, we see examples of corpses being washed, anointed with aromatic preparations, and wrapped in linen cloths or bandages. Lack of burial was the ultimate humiliation. The evil queen Jezebel was left in the street and her flesh eaten by the dogs.

Ancient Cemeteries

Cemeteries have been some of the richest sources of information about life in the ancient world, because bodies were usually buried with important artifacts, and even food. Burials in Palestine were done in sealed caves, in large rock-cut chambers where many bodies were stored, and in burial boxes (ossuaries). The bones of infants were often buried in clay jars.

Anthropoid Clay Coffins

The Egyptians and the Philistines sometimes buried their dead in large clay storage jars. The top third or half of the jar was cut away so that the body could be inserted and the top was then replaced. Over the face, a rough and somewhat grotesque likeness of the deceased was molded in the clay.

Royal Tombs?

The Bible mentions the burial of many of Judah's kings. The earliest kings were buried in the City of David and later ones were buried outside the city. Numerous rock-cut caves exist today that may have been these early tombs, and the later ones were identified in the 1980s in two magnificent burial cave complexes north of the Old City of Jerusalem.

Ossuaries: Burial Boxes

Ossuaries are small clay or limestone boxes used for burial of human bones. Bodies were placed in caves or tombs until they had decomposed enough for the bones to be gathered up and placed in ossuaries for final storage. This was done to make space for more burials and was a very common practice during the New Testament era.

The Bones of a Criminal

The bones of a man named Yehohanan, who was executed by crucifixion, were discovered in 1968 in an ossuary in northeastern Jerusalem. These remains date to the New Testament period. One of the victim's heel bones was pierced by an iron nail, $5^1/2$ inches long, with traces of wood still attached. His forearm bone had what may have been a nail mark in it and his lower legs had been shattered with an ax.

An anthropoid coffin

Woman and Man

Just as in English, the Hebrew words for woman and man are related to each other. Adam called Eve "woman" (Hebrew *ishshah*) because she was taken out of "man" (Hebrew *ish*) (Genesis 2:23).

Adam and Eve in the Garden

Adam: Earth Creature?

Adam's name (Hebrew *Adam*) is related to the word for earth or ground (Hebrew *adamah*). Undoubtedly this involves a play on words, since Adam was formed from "dust from the ground" (Genesis 2:7). Some modern works translate *Adam* as "earth creature" or "earthling" to emphasize this fact.

Eve: Mother of Life

Eve's name in Hebrew (*chavvah*) means "life." Adam called his wife "Eve, because she was the mother of all living" (Genesis 3:20). The word for "living" (Hebrew *chayyah*) is related to Eve's name.

Shortened Life Spans

In the Bible, the long life spans came before the great flood. Methuselah lived for 969 years. After that, very few people lived more than 120 years. Interestingly enough, in the Sumerian King List, which records reigns of thousands of years, the lengths of the reigns also drop dramatically after "the Flood had swept over the earth." The first king, A-lulim, reigned for 28,800 years. After the flood, the reigns of kings were in hundreds of years: 1,200, 960, 840, 600, 400, 140, and so on.

Nimrod: World's First Warrior

Genesis 10:8,9 says of Nimrod, "He was the first on earth to be a mighty man. He was a mighty hunter before the Lord." He had a great kingdom that included several cities in Babylonia and Assyria. The Bible says that he built Nineveh as well.

God tells Abraham that he will have as many descendants as the stars in the sky.

Abraham: Father of a Great Nation

Abraham's original name was Abram, which means "exalted father" or "the father is exalted." God gave him his new name, Abraham, which is explained as "father of a multitude." This was to emphasize God's promise to Abraham that he would have many descendants.

The Curse of Ham

One of Noah's sons, Ham, looked on his father inappropriately when his father was drunk and naked. For this, Noah pronounced a curse on his son. Some people have incorrectly seen Ham as the ancestor of the African peoples and made the wrong assumption that this was a curse on all black people.

Ishmael: Father of the Arabs

Ishmael was the son of Abraham by his wife's maid, Keturah (or Hagar). She was driven away from the household when Sarah's taunting became unbearable (Genesis 16). God promised that Ishmael's descendants would make a great nation also and Arabs generally trace their ancestry back to him. The Quran states that "Abraham and Ismail [Ishmael] built the Kaba [the house of God in Mecca] as the house of God." This was long before the Temple in Jerusalem was built.

Abimelech: Philistine Royal Title?

The stories in Genesis 20 and 26 about Abimelech and the Hebrew patriarchs suggest to many scholars that Abimelech may not have been a personal name, but rather a royal title, just as pharaoh was the title of Egyptian kings. *Abimelech* means "my father is king," which supports this assumption.

Abimelech: Twice Burned?

Genesis 20 and 26 tell similar stories about Abraham and Isaac trying to pass off their wives as their sisters at Gerar, a Philistine city. This was for fear of the Philistine king, Abimelech, who they thought would kill them in order to take their wives. The events were separated by many years, however, and the two Abimelechs may have been different people.

Jacob and Esau: Squabbling Brothers

Jacob and his twin brother, Esau, did not get along well for much of their lives, because Jacob took Esau's birthright. Their descendants were the Israelites and the Edomites, respectively, groups that continued to feud throughout their histories. The Bible states that this feud began even before Jacob and Esau's births: "The children struggled together within her [their mother, Rebekah's, womb]" (Genesis 25:22).

Jacob: A Real Heel

When Jacob and Esau were born, Esau was born first, followed by Jacob, who had hold of Esau's heel. The word "heel" in Hebrew is *aqeb,* and Jacob was named for this: *yaaqob.* His name means "one who grasps by the heel," or "one who restrains."

Jacob Becomes Israel

Jacob wrestled one night with a stranger whom he recognized as God's representative, and he asked him for a blessing. The man then bestowed a new name upon him: Israel. This name means "he strives with God" or "God strives." It is based on a rare Hebrew form for striving (*yisar*) and one of the words for God (*El*).

Jacob wrestles with an angel.

Rachel's Death

Rachel was Jacob's beloved wife, and she bore him Joseph and Benjamin, his two favorite sons. However, she died giving birth to Benjamin. As he was born, she named him *Benoni,* which means "son of my sorrow," but he was renamed Benjamin ("son of the right hand") by his father (Genesis 35).

Rachel's Tomb

Jacob buried his wife Rachel near Ephrath (Bethlehem), and he built a pillar there on her grave, which stood for many years. A domed monument was built in the twelfth century A.D. by the Crusaders near Bethlehem at the traditional site of her grave. Today it is a mosque. Interestingly, bedouins (nomadic Arabs) today bury their children near the tomb.

Moses' Name

Moses' name in Hebrew is based upon the word for "to draw out." Exodus 2:10 explains that he was named "Moses" (Hebrew *Mosheh*) because he was drawn out (Hebrew *mashah*) of the water. In Egyptian, his name was probably *Mose* or *Ramose;* this is similar to many known Egyptian names, such as Ahmose or Thutmose.

Moses and King Tut

Moses grew up in an Egyptian royal household within 100 years of the pharaoh Tutankhamen, whose richly supplied tomb was discovered in 1923. The spectacular finds—including many alabaster vessels, gold-covered objects, and furniture inlaid with gold, ivory, and precious stones—represent things Moses probably had known. Most of the ornamentation in the Israelite Tabernacle would have looked similar, because Egyptian-trained artisans crafted it and the Egyptians gave the Israelites much gold and valuables when the Israelites left for the promised land.

Aaron's rod becomes a snake before pharaoh.

Egyptian Magicians

The Egyptian magicians in Moses' day were able to duplicate the first two plagues that God sent upon Egypt. These were the turning of the water of the Nile River into blood and producing frogs. They tried to duplicate the third plague—bringing forth gnats—but they failed. They also were able to turn their rods into snakes, like Aaron did, but his "snake" devoured theirs.

Achan and the Agony of Defeat

Achan was the man who caused the Israelites their only defeat when they entered the land of Canaan (Joshua 7). When they took Jericho, they were to set aside everything to God for destruction, including all material goods. However, Achan's greed got the best of him, and he hid some goods in his tent. As a result, Israel was defeated in their next battle, at the tiny outpost of Ai.

Ehud: The Left-Handed Judge

Ehud's left-handedness stood him in good stead when he confronted Eglon, the king of Moab (Judges 3). He hid a dagger on his right thigh under his clothes, and used it to kill the king when they were alone together. His left-handedness must have been known; any weapon would have been assumed to be on his left side, so this dagger went undetected on his right side.

Gideon: Saint or Sinner?

Gideon was one of the Bible's heroes: God gave him a great victory over the Midianites (Judges 7). He then properly refused an offer to make him king as a result. However, he was not perfect. He made an ephod (a priestly garment—the high priest wore one) and Israel committed idolatry by worshiping with it. Judges 8:27 states that "it became a snare to Gideon and to his family."

Deborah: A Mother in Israel

Deborah is called "a mother in Israel" (Judges 5:7). In this context, it refers to her leadership over Israel.

Deborah

Israel had been quietly submitting to its enemies in those days, and it was not until Deborah arose as "a mother in Israel" that Israel began to have hope again. She provided the impetus and leadership for action and eventual victory.

Shamgar and Samson: Philistines' Nemeses

Samson was responsible for the death of several thousand Philistines (Judges 14–16). This was helpful to the Israelites, since the Philistines were their major antagonists. Once, he even killed 1,000 men with the jawbone of a donkey. Shamgar was a lesser-known judge, but he too killed many Philistines (Judges 3:31).

Bittersweet Naomi

Naomi, Ruth's mother-in-law, lost her husband and her two sons. Her name means "pleasant," but she told people to call her *Mara,* which means "bitter" (Ruth 1:20). Fortunately, in the end, things were pleasant for Ruth and Naomi.

Ahilud's House

Ahilud was a homeowner in Raddana, near biblical Ai, during the days of Samuel. His house (his name was found inscribed on a jar handle) has been excavated. It was a modest house, with just two long, narrow rooms: One room was 6 feet by 40 feet and the other was 15 feet by 40 feet. Cooking was done outdoors and no bathrooms existed.

Short People

Ahilud and his contemporaries during the biblical period of the judges (about the eleventh century B.C.) were short. Supporting pillars for roof beams in Ahilud's house at Raddana were only five feet three inches tall, and a beam hole in the house wall was also at the same height.

King Mesha, a Strange but Effective Tactician

Mesha, king of Moab, was an enemy of Israel's kings Ahab and Jehoram (2 Kings 3). He paid tribute to Ahab because Ahab was very powerful, but rebelled against Jehoram. When the battle went against him, Mesha sacrificed his oldest son on the wall of the city, in full view of the Israelites, which caused Israel to withdraw.

Delilah: Samson's Lover

Delilah has become famous as a symbol of a treacherous seductress, since she was Samson's lover and the one who betrayed him to the Philistines. She did this by coaxing from him the secret to his great strength, which was his long hair (Judges 16). Contrary to popular thought, she did not cut his hair, but rather held his head on her lap (he was asleep) while the man she called in cut it.

Ichabod: Born Under a Bad Sign

Samuel's daughter-in-law gave birth to a son at a bad time in Israel's history, just after the Ark of the Covenant—which represented God's presence and glory—had been captured by the Philistines. Because of this, she named her son *Ichabod,* which means "there is no glory" (or "where is the glory?").

Unfortunate Agag

Agag was king of the Amalekites whom Saul captured alive and spared (1 Samuel 15). God's instructions had been to kill all the Amalekites, even the king. Samuel summoned the prisoner

Agag, who came cheerfully because he thought and even said, "Surely the bitterness of death is past." Samuel, however, confronted him with his atrocities and then cut him up into many pieces.

Saul and the witch of Endor

Saul and the Medium at Endor

Early in his reign, King Saul had tried to rid the land of the mediums and wizards. However, late in life, when God no longer answered his inquiries, he used the services of a medium to inquire about his upcoming battle with the Philistines. The medium called up Samuel from the dead, who was disturbed at being called, but who prophesied Saul's death.

Jonathan: A Bighearted Man

Jonathan, Saul's son, won an impressive victory over the Philistines at the Pass of Michmash (1 Samuel 14), and he rightfully aspired to succeed his father as king. However, when it became clear that God had rejected his father's claim to the throne and that David would become king, he held no grudge and enthusiastically supported David.

David and Goliath: Test of Champions

When David met Goliath in a one-on-one confrontation, they were engaging in a relatively uncommon "contest of champions." Each army would pick its best warrior to do battle. The winning side was determined by the results of this contest, thereby avoiding much bloodshed and death. However, when David killed Goliath, the Israelites pursued and killed many Philistines.

Goliath's Spear

Goliath's spear is described as being "like a weaver's beam." This meant that it had a leash of cord wrapped around the spear shaft, with a loop into which he inserted his fingers. This was similar to a weaver's beam, which was a block of wood attached to a cord for separating the threads. This styling would have given the spear a spin, and thus a longer and truer trajectory.

Who Were the Nephilim?

The Nephilim were ancient men of great stature and reputation, known only from Genesis 6:4 and Numbers 13:33. Little is known about them except that they were very large (the King James Version translates their name as "giants"). Some scholars think they were the offspring of a supposed union between gods and humans, spoken of in Genesis 6:1–3, but this is doubtful.

The Anakim: Men of the Neck

The Anakim (or Anakites) were pre-Israelite inhabitants of Canaan who posed a great threat to the Israelites when they entered the land. The Anakim were associated with other giants in the land at the time. Numbers 13:33 associates them with the Nephilim. Anakim means "long-necked men" or "men of the necklace." The Egyptian Execration Texts mention three Anakite names.

The Rephaim: Shady Characters

The term "rephaim" is used in many of the Old Testament poetic books to refer to the inhabitants of the shady netherworld beyond the grave (see Job 26:5). It is usually translated as "the dead" or "the shades." The word is also found in many extra-biblical references to those who are dead. The relationship between these and the (living) Transjordanian Rephaim is unclear.

The Rephaim: Great Warriors

The Rephaim were a group of giants from Transjordan who were great warriors. They were defeated by Chedorlaomer, king of Elam, along with several other kings (Genesis 14). They appeared again as giants in the land of Canaan when Israel was set to enter it, as well as in the days of David. The Revised Standard Version renders the Hebrew word rephaim as "giants" when it refers to the men of David's day, and as "Rephaim" when it refers to the earlier inhabitants of Canaan.

Og's Bed: Top-of-the-Line Model

Og, king of Bashan (an area northeast of the Jordan River), opposed the Israelites when they wanted to pass through his land of Bashan (Deuteronomy 3). He was a giant of a man. His bed was made of iron, and it was on display in Rabbah, capital of the Ammonites, for many years. It was more than 13 feet long and 6 feet wide!

Ishbosheth: Man of Shame

2 Samuel 2 calls Saul's son *Ishbosheth,* which means "man of shame." 1 Chronicles 8:33 gives his name as *Eshbaal,* which means "man of Baal." He was probably born as Eshbaal. However, the author of 2 Samuel substituted the name meaning "man of shame," rather than honor a pagan god.

David's Kindnesses to Mephibosheth

David and Jonathan, one of Saul's sons, made a pact that they would remain loyal to each other and each other's posterity (1 Samuel 20). After Jonathan died, David inquired about his relatives. Mephibosheth, who was crippled, was the only one left, so David took him in like a son (2 Samuel 9).

Absalom's hair gets caught in an oak tree.

Absalom: Too Bigheaded for His Own Good

When Absalom—who had revolted against his father, David—was fleeing from some of his father's men, his head got caught in the thick branches of a large oak tree (2 Samuel 18:9). He was stuck fast enough that his servants discovered him hanging there, had a conversation about him, and then one of them decided to kill him, which he did.

Rebellious Sons

Several important characters in the Bible had sons who turned out badly. The two sons of Aaron, the high priest, offered unsanctioned sacrifices (Leviticus 10). The two sons of Eli the priest abused their priestly position and were called "worthless men" (1 Samuel 2). Samuel's two sons took bribes and perverted justice (1 Samuel 8).

David: A Poor Father

The Bible explicitly states that David did not practice good discipline with at least one of his sons. Referring to his son Adonijah, who rebelliously proclaimed himself king, we read "[David] had never interfered with him by asking, 'Why do you behave as you do?'" (1 Kings 1:6). In other words, David was reluctant to call his son to accountability, and he suffered because of it.

Nabal, the Calebite

Nabal was an unfortunate man. His first name means "fool," and his surname means "dog" (dogs were despised creatures in the ancient Near East). Nabal lived up to his name in foolish dealings with David. Eventually, Nabal drank himself to death.

The Duties of a King

Deuteronomy 17:14–20 lists the qualifications and duties of a king. God must choose him, he must be an Israelite, he must not multiply horses for himself (i.e., rely on his army, with its horses and chariots), he must not multiply wives (who might turn his heart away from God), he must not accumulate too much wealth, and he must know and keep the Law.

Solomon: Man of Peace

Solomon's name (Hebrew *Shelomo*) means "peace" (*shalom*), and it reflected God's promises about his kingdom. David was told that he should not build the Temple in Jerusalem, because he was a man of war. Instead, God said, "a son shall be born to you;

he shall be a man of peace. I will give him peace from all his enemies round about; for his name shall be Solomon, and I will give peace and quiet to Israel in his days" (1 Chronicles 22:9).

Who Was Jedidiah?

Jedidiah was another name given to Solomon. It means "beloved of the Lord." After David had sinned by committing adultery with Bathsheba, their child died. A second child (Solomon) was born, and one name David gave him was Jedidiah, since he had been reassured that the Lord had forgiven him and still loved him.

Solomon: Collector of Horses, Women, and Gold

David's son Solomon was a great king in many ways, but he directly violated many of the duties of a king. He amassed great collections of horses and chariots, he took hundreds of wives, and he accumulated immense wealth. All of these were forbidden to a king of Israel.

A "Solomonic Decision"

This phrase refers to a judicial decision in an extraordinarily difficult case that brilliantly reveals the truth or finds some middle ground. It comes from a case Solomon faced, where two women argued over the same baby. His solution was to cut the baby in half. The imposter was happy with this arrangement, but the true mother revealed herself by refusing to let the baby be killed and offering to let the other woman have the baby (1 Kings 3).

The Queen of Sheba visits Solomon.

Solomon and the Queen of Sheba

After she had heard of his fame, the queen of Sheba came from her kingdom in southern Arabia or northeast Africa to test Solomon with hard questions (1 Kings 10). He impressed her with his great wisdom, knowledge, and wealth, so she honored him with huge quantities of expensive gifts.

Jesus and the Queen of the South

In the New Testament, the queen of Sheba is called "the queen of the south" (Sheba was probably in southern Arabia). Jesus referred to her, saying that she had come a long distance to honor Solomon. The implication was that Jesus, being greater than Solomon, was worthy of even greater honor. Jesus said she would arise at the judgment to condemn the evil generation that rejected him (Jesus) instead of honoring him (Luke 11:31).

Hezekiah and Josiah: The Best and the Brightest?

Hezekiah and Josiah were among Judah's greatest kings. 2 Kings 18:5 states that Hezekiah was incomparable: "He trusted in the Lord the God of Israel; so that there was none like him...after him, nor...before him." In 2 Kings 23:25, it is stated that Josiah was incomparable also: "Before him there was no king like him, who turned to the Lord with all his heart...nor did any like him arise after him."

Jehoiachin in Babylon

The Bible records that the last king of Judah, Jehoiachin, was treated humanely in Babylonian exile (2 Kings 25:27–30). The Babylonian king freed him from prison, gave him a prestigious post among captured kings, and invited him to dine daily at the king's table. In this way, the Book of 2 Kings ends with an outlook of hope for the future of God's people.

Mordechai: Jewish Hero With a Pagan Name

Mordechai and Esther are the two heroes of the Book of Esther. Mordechai is honored by the Persian king and placed in the highest position in the land. Ironically, he is named for a Babylonian god, Marduk. It occurs in an extrabiblical list of Persian dignitaries as "Mardukka."

Ramses II: Monumental Builder

Ramses II was one of Egypt's greatest pharaohs, reigning for 67 years in the thirteenth century B.C. Many scholars believe he was the pharaoh during Israel's exodus from Egypt. He built many great temples, including the astounding temple complex built into the sandstone cliffs at Abu Simbel on the Nile River. In the 1960s, when the Aswan Dam threatened this complex, an international rescue effort cut out the temples and relocated them on higher ground.

King Nebuchadnezzar lives like the beasts of the field.

The Long-Haired King

The Book of Daniel tells of King Nebuchadnezzar's being humbled by God. He was driven away from

Babylon into the fields, where he lived with the beasts of the field and ate grass "like an ox, and his body was wet with the dew of heaven till his hair grew as long as eagles' feathers, and his nails were like birds' claws" (Daniel 4:33).

Alexander the Great

Alexander was king of Macedon from 336 B.C. until his death at age 32 in 323 B.C. During this short time, he overwhelmed the eastern Mediterranean and southwestern Asian worlds, establishing a mighty empire stretching from Greece to Egypt to India. After he died, his empire was divided among his four top generals.

Alexander in the Book of Daniel

The Book of Daniel tells of Alexander's empire and its breakup with a remarkably accurate portrayal: "Then a mighty king [Alexander] shall arise, who shall rule with great dominion and do according to his will. And when he has arisen, his kingdom shall be broken and divided…but not to his posterity…for his kingdom shall be plucked up and go to others besides these" (Daniel 11:3,4).

Alexander the Goat

In one of Daniel's visions, he saw an accurate picture of Alexander and his empire. He reports that "a he-goat [Alexander] came from the west…and the goat had a conspicuous horn between his eyes…. Then the he-goat magnified himself exceedingly; but when he was strong, the great horn was broken, and instead of it there came up

287

four conspicuous horns toward the four winds of heaven" (Daniel 8:5–8).

Noah, Daniel, and Job

While making a point about people bearing responsibility for their own sins, Ezekiel stated that even if righteous figures such as Noah, Daniel, and Job were in the land, their righteousness would not rub off onto others (Ezekiel 14:14). Noah and Job were great figures from the past, but Daniel was a contemporary of Ezekiel's. Daniel was exiled to Babylon at an early age, so his reputation for godliness must have spread quickly among the exiles.

Noah builds the ark.

Who Was Danel?

The New English Bible reads "Noah, Danel, and Job" in Ezekiel 14:14. This reflects the judgment that the "Daniel" in the Hebrew text was not Ezekiel's contemporary, but a semilegendary Phoenician king named Danel, known from the Canaanite "Legend of Aqhat." In this way, the three figures would all have been ancient heroes. However, Ezekiel's point about righteousness according to the biblical God's standards would have been diluted had he used such an extrabiblical figure.

Sanballat: Governor of Samaria

Sanballat was the leader of local opposition to Nehemiah's efforts in rebuilding the walls of Jerusalem (Nehemiah 4). An important extra-biblical document found among the Elephantine Papyri on the Nile, dating shortly after the Book of Nehemiah, mentions Sanballat and his sons: "Delaiah and Shelemiah, the sons of Sanballat the governor of Samaria."

Micaiah: Principled Prophet

When kings Ahab and Jehoshaphat wanted to go out to war, they consulted 400 of Ahab's prophets, who told them that God would be with them. Jehoshaphat wanted a second opinion, so they sent for Micaiah. Ahab hated Micaiah, because "he never prophesies good concerning me, but evil" (1 Kings 22:8). True to form, Micaiah formed a minority of one in speaking against Ahab, but his was a true prophecy from God.

Micaiah's Humor

Ahab's 400 false prophets told him to "Go up into battle; for the Lord will give the enemy into your hand" (1 Kings 22:6). Micaiah's first response to Ahab's inquiry was exactly the same, word for word. However, Ahab recognized Micaiah's sarcastic humor, and urged him to tell the truth, which he then did: Micaiah had a message of doom for Ahab.

Did Huldah Go to College?

The King James Version states that the prophetess Huldah lived "in Jerusalem in the college" (2 Kings 22:14). This results from a misunderstanding of the Hebrew term *mishneh* (literally, "second"), which most modern versions translate as "Second Quarter" or "Second District." This area of Jerusalem was on the hill west of the Temple Mount.

Ezekiel: A Real Wordsmith

On 38 occasions, Ezekiel used a very pejorative word for idols in the Old Testament: *gillul*. This word combines the vowels of the word for "sacrilege, abomination" (*shiqqush*) with the consonants of the word for "dung pellets" (*galal*). The resulting word means "idol" (but it is not the usual word for idol), and it expresses a special disgust for these objects.

Amos: Not a Prophet nor a Son of a Prophet

When the prophet Amos protested that he was not a prophet nor a prophet's son (Amos 7:14), he meant that he had not been raised or trained as a prophet, and he did not make his living prophesying. He did not live with other prophets in one of the prophetic schools. Rather, he had his own profession—he was a herdsman and a dresser of sycamore figs—and he was prophesying only because God had sent him on a special mission.

Isaiah: Biblical Streaker

Isaiah walked through the streets of Jerusalem naked and barefoot for three years. He did this to make the point that Egypt and Ethiopia would be taken captive and humiliated, stripped naked and barefoot by the Assyrians (Isaiah 20:2–4).

Cyrus: Pragmatic Politician

Cyrus' famous decree releasing captives to return to their homelands is mentioned in the Bible, but the complete text was discovered in the middle 1800s on a 10-inch-long clay cylinder. In it, Cyrus claims credit from the god Marduk, mentioning his own popularity, and tells of how he freed all people to return to their native lands, asking them to pray to their gods for him.

Sennacherib: Ancient Propagandist

Ancient Near Eastern kings loved to boast about their successes, but they did not write about their defeats. The powerful Assyrian king Sennacherib invaded Judah and besieged Jerusalem in 701 B.C., during Hezekiah's reign. The Bible reports that Sennacherib's army was decimated overnight by "the angel of the Lord." Sennacherib's account of this encounter speaks of "shutting up Hezekiah like a bird in a cage," but he carefully avoids any mention of defeat.

Elijah is taken to heaven in a chariot of fire.

Enoch and Elijah: Two of a Kind

Only two characters in the Bible never died: Enoch and Elijah. Enoch "walked with God" and then "he was not, because God took him" (Genesis 5:24). Elijah the prophet was taken to heaven in a fiery chariot without dying (2 Kings 2).

Elijah and the Prophets of Baal

One of the great confrontations in the Bible was between Elijah and 450 prophets of Baal. They had a contest to see whose god could send down fire on demand. Baal's prophets called upon Baal to no avail. Elijah taunted them, telling them to shout louder, since maybe Baal was thinking, or had turned aside to relieve himself, or had taken a trip, or was asleep (1 Kings 18:27).

Why Baruch Had to Write It Twice

The Book of Jeremiah mentions Baruch, son of Neriah, who was Jeremiah's personal scribe. Jeremiah dictated his book to him. Baruch wrote down Jeremiah's words, but the king destroyed the scroll in anger when it was read to him. Jeremiah then dictated the book all over again.

Something from Baruch's Desk!

A dramatic find was made in the late 1970s. A clay stamp with Baruch's personal seal, with which he would have sealed correspondence and other writing, was discovered. It says "Belonging to Berechyahu [Baruch] son of Neriyahu [Neriah] the scribe." It is one of the only objects ever found that can be personally associated with a biblical character.

Jonadab the Rechabite

Jonadab, ancestor of the ascetic group known as the Rechabites, lived during the days of Ahab, a supremely wicked king of Israel. Jonadab set strict rules for his descendants: They were not to drink wine, build houses, sow seeds, or keep a vineyard. Rather, they were to live nomadic lives in tents (Jeremiah 35).

Hosea: Cuckolded Prophet

God told Hosea to marry a prostitute and to have children with her. God used this to illustrate Israel's prostituting itself by worshiping other gods. To add to Hosea's humiliation, his wife left him for another man, but God told Hosea to take her back. This illustrated God's long-suffering love for his people, no matter what their sins.

Isaiah: Happily Married Prophet

Isaiah calls his wife "the prophetess," and they had two children we know of, both of whose names carried significance for Jerusalem. The first one's name, *Shear-jashub,* means "a remnant shall return." The second child's name, *Maher-shalal-hash-baz,* means "quick pickings, easy prey." Both names foretold the attack of Jerusalem by the Assyrians.

Jeremiah: Bachelor Prophet

God told Jeremiah never to marry or have children, since conditions would soon become so awful in the land that children would die in great numbers and not even be mourned or buried. This was because of the evil that had infested the land.

Ezekiel: Widowed Prophet

Ezekiel's wife, the "delight of his eyes," was taken from him by God, but Ezekiel was instructed not to mourn, weep, or make any public display for her. This was to foreshadow God's destroying the Temple, the "delight of Judah's eyes," which Judah was not to mourn, since Judah had so greatly profaned it and its worship.

Jeremiah prophesies to the king.

Ezra and Nehemiah: Hair-Pullers

Ezra and his contemporary Nehemiah provide a study in contrasting personalities. When Ezra heard that the Jews were marrying foreign women, he tore out his own hair in dismay. On another occasion Nehemiah heard similar news, but, being a more flamboyant type, he tore out the hair of the offenders, not his own!

Malachi: God's Messenger

The Hebrew word *malachi* means "my messenger" and it is also the name of the prophet Malachi. The word is found twice in the Book of Malachi, where it refers once to each, in an obvious play on words.

Who Were the Hasidic Jews?

The Hebrew term *hasidim* means "pious ones," and it is often translated in the Bible as "saints." An identifiable group of Jews called the Hasideans arose during the period between the Old and New Testaments. They resisted the politicalization of the office of high priest during this period, and also the movement toward political independence. Most scholars think the Hasideans were the precursors to the Pharisees.

Modern Hasidism

Modern Hasidism is a religious and social movement that began in the eighteenth century in Eastern Europe. It represented a rebellion against the elite scholarship that had developed in Judaism. Hasidism taught that all could know God equally well, and it emphasized experiential religion, including joyful celebration of life, earnest devotion to God, and even ecstatic experiences. *The Chosen,* a novel made into a movie, sensitively portrays life in a modern Hasidic community.

Melchizedek: King and Priest

Melchizedek was a shadowy figure known mainly from one story in Genesis 14. He was king of Salem (Jerusalem) and "a priest of God Most High." He pronounced a blessing on Abraham, and Abraham gave him a tithe of all he had. A tithe is a tenth, which, under the Law that came later, was to be given to the priests and Levites.

The Ancient of Days

This is a title given to God in Daniel 7, describing the last judgment of the people and the nations. God is described as enthroned on a fiery throne,

King Melchizedek

with snow-white clothing and white hair like pure wool. It is an elegant description for an old man, and it emphasizes God's eternal nature as it contrasts with the earthly kingdoms described in the chapter.

Satan and Lucifer

Many people see a direct reference to Satan in Isaiah's reference to the fallen star (chapter 14). This is partly because the New Testament states "I saw Satan fall like lightning from heaven" (Luke 10:18) and "I saw a star fallen from heaven to earth" (Revelation 9:1). However, the reference in Isaiah is actually to the king of Babylon, who is symbolic of great evil, the ultimate symbol of which is Satan.

The True Morning Star

Christ is called the true "morning star" in the New Testament, in 2 Peter 1:19 ("the morning star rises in your hearts") and Revelation 22:16 ("I am the root and the offspring of David, the bright morning star"). These allusions pick up on such Old Testament passages as Numbers 24:17: "a star shall come forth out of Jacob."

The Angel Gabriel

Gabriel is mentioned only four times in the Bible. Twice he appeared to Daniel to teach him things beyond his comprehension. In the New Testament, Gabriel announced to Zechariah the priest the coming birth of his son, John the Baptist, and he announced to Mary the coming birth of Jesus. *Gabriel* means "God is mighty" or "mighty man of God."

Michael, the Archangel

Michael is an archangel who disputed with Satan in Jude 1:9. Michael's role was less a messenger's (such as Gabriel's) and more an angelic defender's who led armies of angels against the forces of evil. In Revelation 12:7, Michael and his angels fought the great, evil dragon and its forces.

Female Prophets in the Old Testament

Prophetess is used six times in the Old Testament. It refers to Miriam (Exodus 15:20); Deborah

Michael leads the angels to fight the dragon.

(Judges 4:4); Huldah (2 Kings 22:14); Isaiah's wife, "the prophetess" (Isaiah 8:3); and Noadiah, a prophetess who opposed Nehemiah (Nehemiah 6:14). Deborah and Huldah were the most important, since they exercised significant responsibilities.

Prophetesses in the New Testament

Several women prophets are seen in the New Testament. Anna was a prophetess (Luke 2:36), and Philip's four daughters prophesied (Acts 21:9). Women were among those who "spoke in other tongues" on the day of Pentecost (Acts 2:1–4), which fulfilled a prophecy of Joel's that "your sons and your daughters shall prophesy" (Joel 2:28).

Herod: Ruthless Husband, Father, and King

King Herod was a ruthless and unpopular ruler who was put in power by the Romans. He executed dozens of political rivals, including a favorite wife and two of his own sons. This same Herod tried to kill the infant Jesus by ordering a mass slaughter of infants in Bethlehem.

Herodium: A Man–Made Mountain

In 23 B.C., King Herod built a spectacular palace-fortress complex for himself in the wilderness southeast of Jerusalem. A 90-foot-high cylindrical double wall was constructed around the top of a natural hill, and then a sloping fill of earth and gravel added around it, partially burying the wall. This created an impregnable cone-shaped mountain that is visible from Jerusalem, eight miles away. Herod is buried at Herodium, but his tomb has never been discovered.

The Life of Luxury

Herod's Herodium, 200 feet wide, was a most luxurious place. Seven stories of living rooms, storage areas, and cisterns were built, including a complete Roman bathhouse and a beautiful open courtyard in the area below the top of the walls. It was the third largest palace in the Roman world, and by far the most luxurious in Israel. Its wonders were revealed through excavations in the 1960s.

The Pharisees

Jesus had many run-ins with Pharisees, especially about the hypocrisy of some. Because of this, "pharisaical" has come to mean hypocritical or sanctimonious. However, the original impulse of the Pharisees was noble: To follow and obey God's Law in every area of life. Unfortunately, this led to a dry and arrogant legalism in some.

Nicodemus: Pious Pharisee

Nicodemus was a devout Pharisee leader who came to Jesus by night to inquire about Jesus' teachings (John 3). Jesus had an extended discussion with him, and it appears that he became a follower of Jesus, while still remaining a Pharisee. Later, Nicodemus defended Jesus in the Sanhedrin, at some risk to his own reputation (John 7:50–52), and he helped to bury Jesus' body (John 19:39–42).

The Sadducees

Along with the Pharisees, the Sadducees were the major party in Judaism in Jesus' day. They came from a more aristocratic, mostly priestly class, and concentrated more on political affairs than did the Pharisees. They rejected such doctrines as the immortality of the soul, resurrection, or most things having to do with any afterlife.

The Zealots

A small minority of Jews in Jesus' day were Zealots—Jewish revolutionaries. They were radical patriots, and chafed under pagan Roman rule. They constantly agitated against the Romans, and they were responsible for the revolts that led to the destruction of Jerusalem in A.D. 70. One of Jesus' disciples, Simon the Zealot, had been a member.

The Essenes

This was an ascetic group of Jews living in Jesus' day who rigorously observed the Sabbath and other Mosaic laws, including ritual purification (although not animal sacrifice). They worked at agriculture and other pursuits, ate in silence, remained celibate, cared for their elderly, and owned all things in common. Many have suggested that the community of Jews living on the Dead Sea, at Qumran, was an Essene community.

Elizabeth: John the Baptist's Mother

Elisabeth was the mother of John the Baptist, descended from "the daughters of Aaron" (Luke 1:5). Her name was the same as Aaron's wife's (Exodus 6:23); its Hebrew form means "my God is (my) oath" (or "one who worships God"). Luke 1:36 states that Elizabeth was Mary's "kinswoman," a general word meaning relative.

Childless Women in the Bible

Several women in the Bible are described as childless at some point: Sarah, Rebekah, Rachel (all wives of the patriarchs), Samson's mother, Hannah,

John the Baptist's birth

and Elizabeth. Each was given a child in the tradition expressed in Psalm 113:9: "He gives the barren woman a home, making her the joyous mother of children." In biblical times, being childless was a woman's greatest misfortune. David's wife Michal was made barren because of her contempt for his dancing before the Lord.

John the Baptist: A Real Wild Man

John the Baptist, who pointed the way to Jesus and baptized him, lived an ascetic life in the Judean wilderness near the Dead Sea. He survived on simple desert fare, eating whatever the desert provided. His dress was also rustic: He wore a tunic of camel's hair with a leather belt.

Salome: Dancer Extraordinaire

Salome was Herod's brother's daughter. She danced for Herod and upon pleasing him, received his promise to do anything for her. She asked for the head of John the Baptist on a plate, a request prompted by her mother (Matthew 14). Rather than be embarrassed in front of his guests, Herod was forced to follow through on Salome's request.

Jesus' Family: At the Poverty Line

Jesus' family was not wealthy. When his parents brought him to the Temple for the purification ceremony 33 days after his circumcision, they offered a sacrifice of two doves or pigeons, in obedience to the Law. The normal sacrifice for this ceremony, however, was a lamb. Doves or pigeons were only to be offered by those who could not afford a lamb (Leviticus 12:6–8; Luke 2:22–24).

Jesus' Brothers and Sisters

The Bible mentions Jesus' brothers a number of times and his sisters twice. In two passages, several (or maybe all) of his brothers are mentioned, along with his sisters: "Is not this the carpenter's son? Is not his mother called Mary? Are not his brothers James and Joseph and Simon and Judas? And are not all his sisters with us?" (Matthew 13:55,56). They are also mentioned in Mark 6:3.

Who Were Jesus' Brothers?

Three major theories to explain the nature of Jesus' brothers have arisen. One holds that these were step-brothers, Joseph's children by another marriage. A second holds that they were actually his cousins. A third holds that they were true blood brothers (half-brothers). The first two views preserve a doctrine of the perpetual (life-long) virginity of Mary, held in the Roman Catholic and Orthodox wings of the Church, and the third (held by Protestants) does not.

Jesus: A Prophet Without Honor

Early in Jesus' ministry, he had spectacular success, drawing large, appreciative crowds. However, when he went back to his hometown and taught in the synagogue there, people were skeptical. He then said, "A prophet is not without honor, except in his own country," and his ministry there was inhibited (Mark 6:4).

Nicolaitans: Hated by Jesus

The Book of Revelation mentions the Nicolaitans, "whom I [Jesus] hate." They were associated with the teaching of Balaam, who encouraged the Israelites to practice immorality and eat food offered to idols. This was in precise violation of an apostolic decree (Acts 15:20). They may have been followers of Nicolaus, the first Gentile convert. Nicolaus later turned away from his convictions.

Peter the Rock

Peter's name in Greek (*Petros*) means "rock" (*petra*). A climactic point in Jesus' ministry came when Peter confessed that Jesus was the Messiah, the Son of God. Jesus blessed him and said, "You are Peter [*Petros*], and on this rock [*petra*] I will build my church" (Matthew 16:18).

The conversion of Saul

The Bible's Two Sauls

Both men named Saul in the Bible were scoundrels. Saul, the first king of Israel, disqualified himself from being king by his disobedient actions, and he had mental disturbances that caused him to try to kill David several times. Saul of Tarsus was a Jew who persecuted the early Christians. However, he was converted and became the great Apostle Paul!

Peter: Crucified Upside Down?

Christian tradition states that when the Apostle Peter was martyred, he asked to be crucified upside down, since he was not worthy to be crucified in the same manner as his Lord was. This may not have been an unusual mode of crucifixion. Some evidence suggests that condemned criminals may have had their heels nailed together and their legs hung over the top of the cross.

Stoics: Pursuers of Virtue

Acts 17:18 mentions Stoic philosophers who argued with Paul at Athens, where they challenged his view of the resurrection of the dead. Paul even quoted a Stoic poet, Aratus, in his argument (verse 28). Stoic philosophy concentrated upon logic, physics, and ethics. Their ethical striving for virtue is their best-known emphasis, in contrast to the Epicureans, who strove to avoid pain.

Tent–Makers Today

The term "tent-maker" is often used today to describe someone who supports his or her Christian ministry by practicing a trade on the side, as Paul did. Paul argued in 1 Corinthians 9 that Christian workers had every right to be paid by those to whom they ministered, but he personally refrained from claiming this right, so as not to put even the slightest obstacle in the way of his ministry.

Priscilla and Aquila: A Good Team

Priscilla and Aquila were Jews from Corinth who were coworkers with Paul. They instructed Apollos, a gifted teacher, in the ways of Jesus, and they provided hospitality for Paul in their home when he was in Corinth (Acts 18). Priscilla is usually mentioned first, suggesting to some scholars that she may have played the leading role in the couple's ministry in Corinth.

Onesiphorus: Paul's Encourager

Paul had many people who helped and encouraged him in his ministry. One was Onesiphorus, "who often refreshed" Paul. When Paul was imprisoned in Rome, Onesiphorus went to Rome and eagerly looked for him until he found him. There Onesiphorus encouraged him greatly. Paul contrasted Onesiphorus' example with that of Phylegus and Hermogenes, who abandoned him and the Gospel he preached (2 Timothy 1:15–18 and 2:17,18).

Paul and Barnabas: Gods?

When Paul and Barnabas went to Lystra (in Asia Minor, present-day Turkey), they healed a lame man. The crowds were so impressed that they called Barnabas Zeus (the lord of all the Greek gods) and Paul they called Hermes (Zeus' son and spokesman for all the gods), since he was the main speaker of the two (Acts 14:12–17). The people tried to offer sacrifices to them, but the two restrained them from doing so, stating "Friends, why are you doing this? We are mortals just like you, and we bring you

308

Judas betrays Jesus with a kiss.

good news, that you should turn from these worthless things to the living God...."

Judas Iscariot: Betrayer of Jesus

Judas betrayed Jesus to the Jewish authorities for a small sum, 30 pieces of silver (the price of a slave in the Old Testament). His name, *Iscariot,* probably means either "man of the lie" (a traitor) or "dagger bearer" (assassin).

"Which Judas do you want?"

Some six different people in the New Testament were named Judas. One was a brother of Jesus (Matthew 13:55) and he wrote the Book of Jude. Another Judas was a disciple of Jesus. To distinguish that Judas from Judas Iscariot, John 14:22 calls him "Judas (not Iscariot)."

John: A Modest Man

The Apostle John was probably the author of the Book of John, but he is not mentioned by name. Instead, he refers to himself as "the disciple whom Jesus loved" or by some other means. He says this about his own witnessing of Jesus' death: "He who saw it has borne witness—his testimony is true, and he knows that he tells the truth—that you also may believe" (John 19:35).

Barabbas: Freed Prisoner

Barabbas is known only as the criminal Pilate released instead of Jesus. He is described in the Gospels as "a notorious prisoner" (Matthew 27:16), one of "the rebels in prison, who had committed murder in the insurrection" (Mark 15:7), and "a robber" (John 18:40). Pilate used a custom of releasing a prisoner at Passover (which is not otherwise known), and offered the people a choice: Jesus or Barabbas. The people chose Barabbas.

Joseph of Arimathea: Caretaker of Jesus' Body

Joseph of Arimathea (a village in Judea) was a wealthy member of the Sanhedrin who came

forward and offered his own tomb for Jesus' burial
(Luke 23:50–56). He was given Jesus' body and,
with help from Nicodemus, wrapped the body and
buried it. Later outrageous legends state that Joseph
was sent to England by the Apostle Paul, that he
took the Holy Grail there, and that he freed Ireland
from snakes.

"George Washington they're not!"

In popular American mythology, George
Washington confessed to chopping down a cherry
tree by saying, "I cannot tell a lie." Ananias and
Sapphira were husband and wife who sold some
land and donated part of the money to the church.
However, they lied about it, claiming their donation
was the entire amount. For this, they were both
struck dead on the spot (Acts 5).

Caesar, Kaiser Wilhelm, and the Russian Czars

Caesar was the family name of the Julian family of
Rome, whose most famous member was the
emperor Caius Julius Caesar (102 to 44 B.C.). This
family name was passed down to all Roman
emperors until Hadrian (A.D. 117 to 138). The
German word *kaiser* and the Russian word *czar* both
come from Caesar.

"Render unto Caesar"

Some Pharisees tried to trap Jesus by asking him
whether they should pay taxes to Caesar. If he said
yes, they could accuse him of neglecting God's way.
If he said no, he could be accused of subversion of

Roman law. Jesus frustrated them by simply showing them a coin with Caesar's likeness on it and stating, "Render to Caesar the things that are Caesar's, and to God the things that are God's" (Mark 12:17).

Stephen: The First Christian Martyr

Stephen was a deacon, he performed many miracles, and he spoke wise words from God. This displeased many Jewish leaders and trumped-up charges were brought against him. He delivered a long indictment of these leaders, accusing them of complicity in Jesus' death. This enraged the Jewish leaders so much that they interrupted his speech, dragged him outside the walls of the city, and stoned him to death (Acts 6–8).

Philip: First Cross-Cultural Preacher

Philip was one of the seven deacons chosen to minister to Gentile widows, and he was also the first Christian to preach outside of Jerusalem (Acts 8). He preached in Samaria, capital of the hated Samaritans. He was also sent into the desert, where he met an Ethiopian official and taught him about God.

Simon and "Simony"

The English word "simony" refers to the practice of buying or selling ecclesiastical pardons or offices. It comes from Simon the Magician, who, after his conversion, tried to buy spiritual power from the Apostles after he saw them laying hands on people and the people receiving the Holy Spirit (Acts 8).

Peter raises Tabitha from the dead.

Beloved Tabitha, the Seamstress

Tabitha, a disciple of Jesus, died in the city of Joppa when Peter was in a neighboring town. Tabitha was beloved in the community, as she "was full of good works and acts of charity" (Acts 9:36). The widows especially missed her, and they showed Peter many of the garments she had made for them. Peter prayed for her and she was made alive again. Her Greek name was Dorcas; both of her names mean "gazelle."

The First *Christians*

A Christian was a follower of Jesus the Christ (Jesus the Messiah). As the Church grew, the followers of Christ became more noticeable, but it wasn't until several years after Jesus died that the disciples were first called Christians. This happened at Antioch of Syria (Acts 11:26).

A Real Sleepyhead

Eutychus, a young man from Troas, fell asleep one evening while he was listening to a sermon by Paul that lasted well past midnight. Unfortunately, he was sitting in a window on the second floor, and he toppled out and died. Fortunately, however, Paul brought him back to life (Acts 20).

What Was an Apostle?

The Greek word *apostolos* ("apostle") comes from *apostello,* which means "to send." In secular Greek usage, *apostolos* often meant "ship," "fleet," or "naval expedition" (something sent out), but almost never did it mean a person sent. In the New Testament, the meaning was attached to people appointed (or sent) to special functions in the church. Usually it referred to the 12 disciples of Jesus or to Paul.

The Sumerians

The Sumerians flourished in southern Mesopotamia in the third millennium B.C. They are credited with the invention of writing about 3200 B.C., and they produced a long list of literary, historical, and mythological-religious works. They also developed advanced systems of laws, mathematics, and astronomy.

The Egyptians

Egyptian civilization flourished in relative isolation in the long, narrow Nile Valley for almost 3,000 years, until it was overrun by Persians and then Greeks. Its golden age came in the second half of the second millennium B.C., which included the time when Moses lived there. Egyptians built great temples and pyramids (many with Israelites as workers), developed a complex writing system and a great literature, and had a complex religious system emphasizing gods of the dead.

The Hittites

A great Hittite empire flourished in Asia Minor (modern-day Turkey) about 1800 to 1200 B.C. No direct contacts between Israel and this kingdom are mentioned in the Bible, although the Book of Genesis mentions several contacts between the Hebrew patriarchs and "Semiticized" Hittites living in the land of Canaan. The Hittites produced many different literary forms, such as certain treaty forms and historical writings, that find parallels in the Old Testament.

The Philistines' idol is destroyed by God because they stole the Ark.

The Philistines

The Philistines were a mixed group of people living in southwestern Palestine, to which land they gave their name. Most of them entered Palestine about 1200 B.C., and they became Israel's major adversaries during the period of the judges and the early monarchy. The Philistines held a monopoly of iron technology for a time, which gave them an advantage in war. David, however, put an end to their domination of Israel about 1000 B.C.

The Arameans

The Arameans occupied a small kingdom northeast of Israel (in present-day Syria). It arose about 1100 B.C. and was often in conflict with Israel over the next four centuries, until it was overrun by Assyria. Their language, Aramaic, became the international language of diplomacy and trade in the Near East during most of the first millennium B.C.

The Canaanites and Amorites

The term Canaanite refers in the Bible to the land area of Syria-Palestine and to various peoples living within that area. Amorite is usually synonymous with Canaanite. The culture and religion of the Canaanites were the greatest threats to Israel's national and religious identity. The Israelites were constantly tempted by them, leading to repeated condemnations of Israel by the prophets.

The Moabites

Moab was a small kingdom east of the Dead Sea. The people of Moab can be traced to Lot, Abraham's nephew. Moabites are seen periodically in the Old Testament skirmishing with the Israelites, until their destruction by Nebuchadnezzar in 586 B.C. The Moabite king Mesha had dealings with the Israelite kings Omri and Ahab that are recorded in the Bible. These dealings were also inscribed on the famous Moabite Stone.

The Ammonites

The Ammonites were distant cousins of the Israelites. They were also descended from Lot,

David punishes the Ammonites.

Abraham's nephew. They lived in a small kingdom east of the Jordan River, in modern-day Jordan. Amman, Jordan's capital, takes its name from the Ammonites. They had regular conflicts with Israel and Judah, and the Israelite prophets roundly condemned the Ammonites and their behavior.

The Phoenicians

The Phoenicians lived in city-states along the Mediterranean coast in what is modern-day Lebanon. The Bible usually refers to them as Canaanites. They distinguished themselves as seafarers, plying the Mediterranean and the coasts of Africa and Europe in their sailing ships. King Hiram of Phoenicia was friendly to kings David and Solomon, helping greatly with the building of the Temple in Jerusalem in Solomon's day. The Phoenician alphabet forms the basis of the Greek alphabet.

The Edomites

The Edomites, descended from Esau, lived in a small desert land southeast of the Dead Sea. They frequently clashed with the Israelites. Their delight in the fall of Jerusalem (Psalm 137:7) was condemned by the prophet Obadiah. The rock-cut city of Petra was built in this area many years after the Edomites lived there.

The Assyrians

The Assyrians lived in the upper Mesopotamian plain (modern-day Iraq) for more than two thousand years before their empire fell to Babylonia in 612 B.C. The height of Assyrian power was in the eighth and seventh centuries B.C. They amassed great armies, made wide-spread conquests, built great cities, and collected great libraries. They toppled the kingdom of Israel in 722 B.C. and reduced Judah to a vassal state.

The Babylonians

Babylonia was a small area in southern Mesopotamia, along the Euphrates River, and it was inhabited since at least 4000 B.C. The kingdom flourished early in the second millennium B.C. under King Hammurabi. Babylonia reached its greatest power in 626 to 539 B.C., when it was toppled by Persia. Babylonian civilization was greatly advanced. They kept impressive literary, historical, legal, mathematical, and astronomical records. Babylonia destroyed Jerusalem in 586 B.C.

The Persians

The Persian empire existed from 559 to 332 B.C., when it was toppled by Greeks under Alexander the Great. At its height, it stretched from India to Greece. Persian kings had a reputation for dealing humanely with captives. They released the Jews to return to Jerusalem, and Jews under Ezra, Nehemiah, and Esther fared well under Persian rule. The dualistic Zoroastrian religion arose in Persia.

The Greeks

Greece was more of a collection of city-states than an empire, although Alexander the Great was a Greek (Macedonian) general. Its major contributions were cultural. It contributed a common language for international discourse, and developed great traditions of speculative philosophy and republican government. The New Testament was written in Greek, and the Apostle Paul preached in many Greek cities, including Athens.

Paul is held prisoner in Rome.

The Romans

The Roman empire grew to encompass the entire Mediterranean basin during the time of Jesus. Roman contributions were primarily architectural (excellent roads, buildings, theaters, gymnasiums, and aqueducts) and political. The Romans had a loose provincial system, under which much local autonomy was allowed, and Roman citizens had many rights. The *Pax Romana* ("Roman Peace"), despite its occasional ruthlessness, allowed for the rapid and peaceful spread of the Christian faith in the decades after Jesus lived.

A Truly "Dead" Sea

Because of its high concentrations of salt and other minerals, no fish can live in the Dead Sea. That is how it got its name. It is nestled in a hostile, barren valley with very few plants surrounding it, but there is an oasis or two. Its southern shoreline is dotted with strange geological formations that make it look like a moonscape.

Salt formations on the Dead Sea

The Lowest Place on Earth

The lowest point on the face of the earth is the surface of the Dead Sea. It is about 1,300 feet below sea level. The Dead Sea is part of the Great Rift Valley that runs north and south through eastern Africa. This valley includes the Jordan Valley to the north of the Dead Sea and parts of the Red Sea to the south.

The Saltiest Sea

One of the Bible's terms for the Dead Sea is the Salt Sea. The Jordan River runs into the Dead Sea, but after that, there is no outlet for the water. The water level stays the same because of evaporation. As a result, the mineral content is very high. This makes it the saltiest body of water in the world—so dense you can't sink. Everyone floats on the Dead Sea!

Lot's Wife

As Lot and his wife fled the destruction of Sodom and Gomorrah, Lot's wife turned to look back and was turned into a pillar of salt. The towering salt cliffs of Jebel Usdum (Mount Sodom) and the salt pillars at the southern end of the sea have been associated in tradition with this event. One distinctive 60-foot-high pillar is even called Lot's Wife.

The Day of the Snow

Snow was (and is) rare in the lands of the Bible, limited mainly to the high mountain ranges. Only one time is an actual snowfall mentioned, but it was remembered in the same way that today we would

Lot's Wife formation

remember outstanding storms ("the tornado of '86"). One of King David's warriors killed a lion "on the day of the snow" (2 Samuel 23:20).

Which Way Is Which?

The Hebrews' mental maps of the world were oriented with the top to the east, not to the north. The Hebrew word for east literally means in front of, while one of the Hebrew words for west means behind. Similarly, south literally means at the right side, and north means at the left side.

The Medeba Mosaic Map

A large mosaic map at Medeba, south of Amman, Jordan, is the oldest map of Palestine, dating to the sixth century A.D. It was 77 feet by 20 feet, made of 2.3 million colorful and tightly fitted stone cubes. Unfortunately, more than two-thirds of it was destroyed in 1896. The remains show many valuable features of sixth century Palestine, including a detailed map of Jerusalem, with the Church of the Holy Sepulcher highlighted.

Ancient Roads

Road and paths in biblical times were usually just dirt tracks, which became impossibly muddy during rainy seasons. Sometimes armies made sturdier roads so they could travel more easily. The pathways of the dirt roads kept changing, however, as caravans searched for smoother ground to cross.

Roman Roads

The Romans built very impressive road systems throughout their empire. The first and most famous was the Appian Way, begun in 312 B.C. It was 15 feet wide and 350 miles long, made with smooth paving stones. The well-preserved remains of this road can still be seen today.

A Roman milestone

One More Milestone for Israel

The Romans used distinctive milestones to mark distances on their roads. These were small, round stone columns set on bases by the sides of the roads. The Romans were master engineers, building extensive networks of good roads throughout their empire, along which the Apostle Paul and others traveled. The roads were built using large slabs of stone. Many of these, including the milestones, are still on Israel's roads today.

Looking for Noah in All the Wrong Places?

Many modern-day expeditions have searched for Noah's ark on the snow- and glacier-covered slopes of Mount Ararat, a 17,000-foot peak in Armenia, in eastern Turkey. However, the Bible says that the ark came to rest on "the mountains of Ararat" (Genesis 8:4), which may mean anywhere in mountainous Armenia.

The Cilician Gates

The Apostle Paul traveled throughout Asia Minor (modern Turkey), and he would have seen some spectacular scenery along the way. Near his hometown of Tarsus in southeastern Asia Minor was the Taurus mountain range, which completely blocked off east-west travel. The one route through these mountains was through the Cilician Gates, a deep, narrow pass through wild, rugged terrain.

Mesopotamia and Hippopotami

Mesopotamia was the fertile region of land between the Tigris and Euphrates rivers, in present-day Iraq, and was the home of the ancient Sumerian, Babylonian, and Assyrian empires. Its name means "the land between (*meso*) the rivers (*potamoi*)." The word hippopotamus is related: It means "river (*potamos*) horse (*hippus*)."

Biblical Deserts

Palestine is bordered by two great deserts. The great Arabian Desert stretches out to the east and southeast and the Sinai Desert is to the south. Within Israel itself, the southern part is called the Negev Desert and the area east of Jerusalem is the wilderness of Judea. It is hilly, but it is dry and parched like a desert.

What? No Sand Dunes?!

For the most part, deserts in Bible lands do not have the great shifting sand dunes that are found in many deserts. Most of these deserts are dry, flat, and rocky. The hot desert winds blow fine dust or sand across the barren surface. Occasionally oases with springs and palm trees can be found.

Life in the Desert

As is even true today, desert dwellers built their lives around raising sheep and goats, which provided dairy products and meat. These animals also provided materials for clothing and for their tents. A major concern in the desert was finding water, so many wells were dug and people found oases. Year-round streams or rivers were not common, but in the rainy season there were many.

Streams in the Desert

Oases were well known in biblical times. The Israelites stayed at the oasis of Kadesh-barnea, in the

En-Gedi

northern Sinai Desert. The famous site of En-Gedi,
the location of a perennial spring in the Judean
wilderness near the Dead Sea, is mentioned several
times in the Bible. A beautiful waterfall cascades
down several hundred feet from this spring, which
is a popular resort center today.

The Navel of the Earth

Many ancient Near Eastern societies developed the concept of their cities or land being at the center of all things—the "navel" of the earth. In the Bible, two places—Shechem, near the religiously significant Mount Gerizim, and the land of Israel itself—are so called. Most English versions today translate the Hebrew phrase as middle (or center) of the earth.

Mount Zion: The Highest of All Hills

The term Mount Zion originally referred to the low hill of Jerusalem on which King David built his early city. Later, it was transferred to the higher hill to the west. It came to symbolize the capital of God's kingdom, and Isaiah and Micah spoke of Mount Zion as ultimately being established as "the highest of the mountains...raised above the hills."

A Blast of Hot Air

The prophet Amos speaks of God roaring like a lion from Jerusalem because he is angry with the nation of Israel and the blast of his roar causing the top of Mount Carmel to wither. Mount Carmel is a lush, wooded mountain more than 70 miles north of Jerusalem. God's breath not only reaches Carmel, but it scorches the shepherd's pastures between these two points as well (Amos 1:2).

Staying Close to Home

Jesus spent almost all of the first year and a half of his public ministry in the region of Galilee, where he grew up. Many important highways passed through Galilee, going to distant places. Thus, Jesus could have had easy contact with a wide variety of people without traveling very far and without exposing himself early in his ministry to the anger of the religious authorities in Jerusalem.

Heavenly Jerusalem— Bigger than a Rubik's Cube

In the Apostle John's vision of heavenly Jerusalem (Revelation 21 and 22), he saw a shimmering, bejeweled city descend from heaven. The city was a spectacular fantasy, however, since it was a perfect cube measuring 1,500 miles on each side—the distance from New York City to Houston. It had a miniature wall totally out of proportion to the other dimensions. It was clearly symbolic of the glories that lay ahead.

Down to Jericho

The Good Samaritan is said to have gone down from Jerusalem to Jericho. This doesn't mean that Jericho is south of Jerusalem (it's east), and it doesn't imply that Jericho was a step down from Jerusalem in wealth, urban development, or status. Jericho is 3,300 feet lower than Jerusalem, an amazing drop for a journey of only 15 miles!

Jerusalem: An Out-of-the-Way Place

Jerusalem was not easy to get to. It was not located on either of the major north-south trade or military routes, the coastal "Way of the Sea," or the eastern "King's Highway" on the Plains of Moab. So, even though tiny Israel was constantly being squeezed

The road from Jericho to Jerusalem

between the world's large empires on either side of it and powerful foreign armies frequently marched through it on their missions of conquest, Jerusalem remained relatively secure as Israel's capital.

Jerusalem: City of Shalom

When the Israelites took over Jerusalem, they were offended by its many gods and pagan culture, and so they gave its name a new meaning, "City of Peace" (*Shalom*). This was possible because its name sounds just like the Hebrew words for "city of peace." This title has remained a symbol of people's hopes for the city ever since.

Hell on Earth

The Hinnom Valley in Jerusalem was a place where residents burned their rubbish. Child sacrifices may have taken place here. As a result, it gained a reputation as a place of fiery abominations and it even came to be symbolic of hell. Its Hebrew name—*ge'hinnom*—formed the basis for the New Testament word *gehenna,* which means "hell."

Holy Rubble

Garbage disposal was a problem even in ancient times. Jerusalem had one valley running down the center of the city just west of the Temple Mount. This valley was called the Valley of the Cheesemakers and it has all but disappeared in modern times. It was filled with rubble over the centuries from successive destructions of the city, and so today it is 115 feet higher than it was. It is now 98 feet west of its location in the days of Jesus.

A Hidden Water Tunnel

The Jebusites who lived in Jerusalem before King David were responsible for an ingenious tunnel system that brought fresh water into their city from the hidden spring in the valley below. They tunneled straight down through the hill above the spring and tapped into an underground stream. They would lower buckets and fill them from this stream and not have to go outside the city walls.

The City of David

The city that David captured from the Jebusites and lived in was small, about 15 acres in size. It was a walled city built on a low, elongated hill, next to which was a hidden spring. It was a significant city despite its size, and David was able to use many of the existing buildings.

How David Captured Jerusalem

Jerusalem's water supply was its weak point, and David exploited it in capturing the city. He challenged his men to "strike at the water shaft," which they did, either by cutting off the water supply or by going up the tunnel itself into the city (2 Samuel 5:7–9).

Tourists at David's Tomb

Tourists in Jerusalem can see the Tomb of David on the southwestern hill, which is today called Mount Zion. However, this tomb dates no earlier than the ninth century, some 1,800 years after David. His actual burial place is unknown.

Water Through a Rock

One of the great engineering feats recorded in the Bible was the 1,750-foot-long tunnel—through bedrock 150 feet under the City of David in Jerusalem—that was dug during King Hezekiah's reign. Its purpose was to direct water inside the city walls from a hidden spring, thus providing a reliable water source in time of siege. It was laboriously hacked out of the rock with pickaxes by two crews digging toward each other.

Let's Meet in the Middle!

A 2,500-year-old inscription carved into stone was found in 1880 near the south end of Hezekiah's water tunnel. The inscription tells the proud story of the climactic labors of its construction crews. It tells of the stonecutters swinging their pickaxes, and then of the excitement of hearing the other workers: "the voice of a man calling to his fellow." They soon were able to meet: "The quarrymen hewed the rock, each man toward his fellow, ax against ax, and the water flowed from the spring toward the reservoir."

Who Is Buried in Absalom's Tomb?

The old joke about who is buried in Grant's tomb takes on new meaning in Jerusalem. A five-story-high monolith cut out of the rock in the hillside east of the Old City of Jerusalem, into which a small burial chamber has been cut, is called Absalom's Tomb. However, Absalom, a son of David, is not buried here. This tomb was cut near the time of Christ, 1,000 years after Absalom lived. It probably got its name because of a biblical reference to a monument that Absalom built for himself.

Jesus Before Pontius Pilate

Pilate, the Roman governor of Judea, pronounced judgement on Jesus at a place called the Pavement, and in Hebrew, *Gabbatha* (John 19:13). This was probably in the Antonia, a massive fortress with four impressive towers at the northwest corner of the Temple Mount. The fortress was built by Herod. The Apostle Paul was also imprisoned there. A large stone pavement, more than 150 feet square, can be seen today under a convent in this area.

Jesus before Pilate

Get Me if You Can!

King Herod (37–4 B.C.) fortified Jerusalem by
building huge walls and high towers around the city.
A three-tower complex defended his palace. The
base of one of these towers, named Phasael's Tower,
can still be seen today. It is an impressive 60-foot
cube, and is popularly, but erroneously, known as

David's Tower. It had been 150 feet high! Herod's grandson, Agrippa I, built 90 additional towers in Jerusalem's outer walls.

Where Did Jesus Die?

Jesus died at a place called *Golgotha,* which is Aramaic for "skull," but its exact location is disputed. Gordon's Calvary is a hill with caves, and its openings make it resemble a skull; however, these caves are artificial excavations only two to three centuries old. Many scholars believe that the present-day Church of the Holy Sepulcher marks the true site of Golgotha.

Where Was Jesus Buried?

Jesus was buried in a rock-cut tomb sealed with a large stone. Many such tombs are known from Jesus' time, with large, circular stones set on edge to cover the entrance. The Garden Tomb near Gordon's Calvary is thought by some to be the site of Jesus' burial, but it is possible the tomb is somewhere under the present-day Church of the Holy Sepulcher.

The Mount of Olives

The Mount of Olives is a graceful hill just across the Kidron Valley from Jerusalem, to the east. Even today it is dotted with olive groves. Jesus spent much time there in the last weeks of his life. He wept when he saw Jerusalem from it as he returned for the last time, he prayed in the Garden of Gethsemane there, he was also arrested there, and from there he ascended to heaven.

Jesus' Footprints?

The Chapel of the Ascension on the Mount of Olives supposedly marks the spot where Jesus ascended to heaven. It was built during Crusader times (in the eleventh century) over a spot marked since the fourth century. A stone slab contains what some claim are Jesus' last footprints on earth.

Abraham's Rock?

A large rock measuring 58 feet long by 51 feet wide by 4 to 6 feet high sits squarely in the middle of the Temple Mount. Different traditions say that this is the rock upon which Abraham offered his son Isaac as a sacrifice, where the great altar of Solomon's Temple stood, and from where Mohammed ascended to heaven. Today, the great Muslim Dome of the Rock stands over the spot.

The Dome of the Rock

A magnificent golden-colored dome dominates the view of the Old City in Jerusalem today. It sits atop an eight-sided building built over the large rock that is significant in both Jewish and Muslim traditions. The first Muslim dome was built in the seventh century A.D., shortly after the Arab capture of Jerusalem in A.D. 638.

Akeldama: Field of Blood

Akeldama was the Aramaic name, meaning "field of blood," given to the field bought with the 30 pieces of silver that Judas received when he betrayed Jesus. The name seems to be due to two reasons: the spilling of Judas' blood (Acts 1:18,19), and the fact that the field was bought with "blood money" (from Jesus' betrayal) (Matthew 27:6). Today, residents of Jerusalem still say they can identify the field.

Judas' Tainted Money

Deuteronomy 23:18 states that "You shall not bring the fee of a prostitute or the wages of a male prostitute into the house of the Lord...for...these are abhorrent to [him]." In accordance with this principle, the priests did not put Judas' 30 pieces of silver into the Temple treasuries, since it was "blood money." Instead, they purchased a field to bury strangers in, called potter's field.

Islamic and Jewish Art: Close Cousins

The most distinctive feature of Islamic religious art is its abstract nature: No living creatures are represented. Exquisite examples of this are found on the walls of the Dome of the Rock, and on the underside of the great dome itself. This prohibition against representing living things is similar to (but stricter than) the Jewish prohibition against making any representations of God himself.

Jerusalem: A Holy City for Three Faiths

Jerusalem is holy to Jews, Christians, and Muslims alike. For Jews, it was the site that David chose as his capital city and where the Temple was built. For Christians, it was where Jesus ministered, died, rose again, and ascended to heaven. For Muslims, it was the place from which the prophet Mohammed was transported to heaven.

Jericho: The World's Oldest City

A fine spring waters Jericho, which was first occupied in 9000 B.C. It was an oasis in the Jordan Valley, and was called the City of the Palms in the Bible. The Israelites captured it under Joshua, in the famous incident when its walls collapsed. It lay as a sparsely inhabited ruin for more than 1,000 years, when it was rebuilt by King Herod.

A Curse Fulfilled

Joshua's curse on the city of Jericho stated that anyone rebuilding Jericho would pay a stiff price (Joshua 6:26): "At the cost of his first-born shall he lay its foundation, and at the cost of his youngest son shall he set up its gates." Many years later, a man named Hiel, from Bethel, did some rebuilding, but it cost him his oldest and youngest sons (1 Kings 16:34), in fulfillment of this prophecy. Today, there is an Arab town called Jericho, but it is not built on the biblical site.

Thebes: City of Temples and Tombs

The Egyptian city of Thebes flourished during the latter half of the second millennium B.C., when Moses and the Israelites were in Egypt. Several magnificent temples were built there, and the Valley of the Kings burial tombs were nearby. The Book of Nahum mentions Thebes' destruction.

Ebla: A Major Discovery

Ebla was the capital of an important Semitic kingdom in northern Syria during the third millennium B.C. Its significance was not realized

until after 1975, when a major cache of thousands
of documents was found there. Ebla was a large city,
a major commercial center, and these texts have
shed light on many aspects of ancient life in the
earliest biblical times.

Ugarit: Great Canaanite City-State

Ugarit flourished on the northeastern
Mediterranean coast in the fourteenth and
thirteenth centuries B.C., close to the time that the
Israelites entered the land of Canaan. Its discovery
in 1929 revealed first-hand texts of Canaanite
religion, including the worship of Baal. Many
Ugaritic texts are poetic, in a language and style
similar to that of the biblical psalms.

Nineveh: Assyrian Capital

Nineveh, on the Tigris River, reached its height of
glory as Assyria's capital under Sennacherib and
Ashurbanipal. Sennacherib built a fabulous palace
with more than 71 rooms, 10,000 feet of sculptured
walls, and 27 gateways formed by huge winged bulls
and sphinxes. Ashurbanipal's palace contained
uncounted treasures of sculpture and art work, and
a library with thousands of texts.

Babylon: Destroyer of Jerusalem

Babylon had a long history, extending into the
postbiblical period. Its greatest glory came in the
seventh and sixth centuries B.C., during which time
it also captured Jerusalem. It had a 280-foot-high
pyramid-shaped temple tower that may have been
the biblical Tower of Babel, along with many other

The Tower of Babel

impressive temples. Thousands of religious and mythological texts have been recovered from Babylon, as well as extremely accurate historical records.

Alexandria: Greek Center of Learning

Alexandria was founded by Alexander the Great in 331 B.C., in the western Nile Delta in Egypt. It soon became a great intellectual, cultural, commercial, and scientific center for many centuries following. It housed a library of 480,000 volumes at one time. It was here that Greek-speaking Jews translated the Hebrew Bible into Greek, making it accessible to thousands of readers, including the writers of the New Testament.

Rome: Oppressor and Nurturer of Christianity

Rome was founded in 753 B.C., and it became the capital of one of the greatest empires of the ancient world. Its systems of government and communication allowed for the rapid spread of Christianity after Jesus' death. The Apostle Paul's great desire was to take the Gospel message to Rome, from which Christianity was to spread throughout the world. Rome was also a symbol of great evil in the New Testament.

Corinth: The Las Vegas of the Roman Empire

Corinth was an important Greek city, located on the isthmus joining the Pelopponesian Peninsula to mainland Greece. It was an important commercial center, and the Apostle Paul chose to establish a church there because of its strategic importance. Corinth in Paul's time was an extremely decadent city, as his letters to the Corinthian church show.

Where Was Tarshish?

The Book of Jonah states that Jonah took a ship going to Tarshish rather than go to Nineveh, as God had commanded him. Tarshish was either part of the island of Sardinia (off the coast of Italy) or a region in far-off Spain. It is obvious that Jonah's intent was to go far away from Nineveh.

Nineveh's Library

A vast library of more than 26,000 clay tablets was discovered at Nineveh in the 1850s in the palaces of Sennacherib and Ashurbanipal. This was the most important find for deciphering the languages of Assyria, and they have provided invaluable insight into its history and culture. The tablets were very carefully numbered and catalogued in series.

Fish Stories: Jonah and Nineveh

A delightfully ironic connection between Jonah and Nineveh can be seen through the fish imagery. Jonah found himself enclosed within the walls of a great fish's belly because he refused to go to Nineveh, which was known as the great fish city that was enclosed within its own walls.

Petra: City in the Cliffs

The ancient city of Petra (probably biblical Sela) is a spectacular city of temples, tombs, buildings, and monuments carved deep into the rock cliffs of a long, narrow gorge in the desert east of the Dead Sea. It was settled by the Nabateans, a people who lived there beginning in the fourth century B.C., and it rose to become an important commercial center.

Petra's "Treasury of the Pharaoh"

The most magnificent monument at Petra is the *Khazneh Far`un,* the "Treasury of the Pharaoh." It is a great temple carved deep into the breathtaking reddish-pink sandstone, with impressive columns and other ornate carvings. Even Hollywood has discovered Petra! The third film of the Indiana Jones series was filmed there.

The Bible's Earthquakes

The Bible mentions three actual earthquakes. One was during the reign of Uzziah (Amos 1:1), another was on the day of Jesus' crucifixion just after he died (Matthew 27:51–53), and a third occurred when Paul and Silas were imprisoned at Philippi (Acts 16:26). This last earthquake broke open the doors of the prison so that prisoners could have escaped, causing the jailer great distress. Paul and Silas, however, reassured the jailer that everyone was still there.

Solar and Lunar Eclipses

The Bible mentions eclipses several times, as prophetic signs of God's judgment. Amos 8:9 states that "I will make the sun go down at noon, and darken the earth in broad daylight." Joel 2:31 says that "The sun shall be turned to darkness, and the moon to blood." Lunar eclipses do indeed look red at times, due to refraction of the sun's light.

The Great Rift Valley

The Great Rift Valley that runs north and south in eastern Africa extends north into Bible lands. It forms the Jordan Valley basin, which includes the Sea of Galilee, the Jordan River, and the Dead Sea. It is the joining point for two great tectonic plates that slowly slide past each other. Zechariah 14:4 mentions the Mount of Olives being split in two, "so that one half...shall withdraw northward, and the other half southward."

Rain and Drought

Life in Palestine depended heavily on rain, in contrast to Egypt and Mesopotamia, where great river systems provided water for crops. Without rain, drought set in and famine was just around the corner. The highest Canaanite god, Baal, was the god of the storms. People wanted to please him, since they thought he could send rain.

The *Khamsin:* Hot East Wind

A hot south and east wind blows across Egypt and Palestine during the months of May and October. It fills the air with a yellow haze of dust and often lasts three days or more. The Bible mentions this wind many times as a symbol of God's wrath. Isaiah 27:8 states that God removed his people into exile "with his fierce blast in the day of the east wind."

Biblical Caves

Caves were abundant in Palestine. They were used as dwelling places (Genesis 19:30), as hiding places (1 Samuel 22:1), and as burial places (John 11:38). The most common types of caves were formed by the action of underground water, where the water table eventually receded and left a cave. The dryness of many caves made them ideal for storage. The Dead Sea Scrolls survived almost two thousand years in caves, without much deterioration.

The Cave of Machpelah

This was the cave that Abraham bought to bury his wife Sarah in, near Hebron (Genesis 23). Abraham, Isaac, and Jacob also were buried there. Abraham's purchase was significant, since it represented the first clear title to the land that God had promised him. A Muslim mosque marks the spot of this cave today.

The Pass of Michmash

Michmash was a town southeast of Bethel where Saul and Jonathan had an encounter with the Philistines (1 Samuel 13,14). The Philistines guarded the narrow pass, but Jonathan and his armor-bearer scaled the cliffs and launched a surprise attack. They killed 20 men and routed the Philistines.

The Garden of Eden: A Biblical Paradise

The Garden of Eden was the lush paradise where God placed the first man and woman. Genesis 2:8 speaks of Eden as a land in which the garden was placed, however: "And the Lord God planted a garden in Eden, in the east." Several passages speak of it as "the garden of the Lord."

The Seven Wonders of the Ancient World

The seven wonders of the ancient world come from the lists of Antipater of Sidon and Philon of Byzantium, travelers in the late pre-Christian era. The wonders are the Great Pyramid at Giza (Egypt), the Hanging Gardens of Babylon, the Statue of Zeus at Olympia (Greece), the Temple of Diana at Ephesus (Asia Minor), the Mausoleum (tomb) at Halicarnassus (Asia Minor), the Colossus of Rhodes (Aegean Sea), and the Pharos (Lighthouse) at Alexandria (Egypt).

The Sphinx guards the pyramid at Giza.

The Great Pyramid at Giza

The Great Pyramid was built as a tomb for the Egyptian pharaoh Khufu at Giza, near modern-day Cairo (about 2700 B.C.). It contains nearly two and a half million stone blocks, each weighing at least two and a half metric tons. It covers an area of 13 acres, and originally rose 481 feet high. It is the only ancient wonder still surviving today. It had already stood for centuries when Joseph and Moses lived in Egypt.

The Hanging Gardens of Babylon

These gardens were built some time in the eighth to sixth centuries B.C. They did not actually hang, but were roof gardens laid out on a series of terraces and were irrigated by pumps, reaching about 350 feet high. The water trickled down over the terraces, but did not seep through, since the stone balconies were roofed with reeds, bitumen, and lead. The Jews exiled in Babylon would have been impressed by the sight of these.

The Statue of Zeus at Olympia

A huge figure of Zeus, the Greek storm god and head of the pantheon, stood 40 feet high in a great temple of Zeus at Olympia, in Greece. It was sculpted about 456 B.C. out of wood, with thin plates of gold and ivory completely covering it. Its eyes were large jewels and its robes were covered with precious stones.

The Mausoleum at Halicarnassus

A brilliant white marble tomb, built by King Mausolus (hence mausoleum) for his wife Atremesia in the fourth century B.C., stood on a hill overlooking the Greek port of Halicarnassus. It stood 140 feet high and was covered by a pyramid dome. Sculptured horses and lions adorned its courtyards and roof. A colony of Jews lived at Halicarnassus in the second and first centuries B.C.

The Temple of Diana at Ephesus

Diana was the Roman name for the Greek goddess Artemis, whose principal shrine was a great temple at Ephesus, on the coast of Asia Minor. The Ephesian Artemis was the goddess of fertility. This magnificent temple was said by Philon to be the greatest of the seven wonders. It was built of white marble and overlaid with gold, silver, and jewels. It had 127 columns, each representing a king. This temple is mentioned in Acts 19:35.

The Colossus of Rhodes

This was a 105-foot bronze statue of the sun god Helios, built in 280 B.C. on the island of Rhodes, in the Aegean Sea. It was built to commemorate a great victory. But 56 years later, it was toppled by an earthquake. The Apostle Paul stopped at Rhodes on his final journey to Jerusalem, but the statue would have lain in ruins on the ground then.

The Pharos at Alexandria

This immense lighthouse was built on the island of Pharos near Alexandria, Egypt, in the third century B.C. It stood more than 400 feet high, had 300 rooms, and held a fire that burned day and night at the top. A huge mirror reflected the light. The Jews who translated the Hebrew Bible into Greek at Alexandria would have seen this great structure.

The Fertile Crescent

The Fertile Crescent is a large arc that encompasses the fertile river valley system of the Tigris and Euphrates rivers in Mesopotamia. It then curves northwest and south to include the eastern seaboard of the Mediterranean (Palestine), and, by some definitions, the Nile River Valley in Egypt.

The Island of Rhodes

Rhodes is a small island just off the southwest coast of Asia Minor, in the Aegean Sea. It was an important commercial center for traders, as it sat astride the shipping routes between the Aegean and the eastern Mediterranean. It did not have natural wealth of its own. Ezekiel mentions its trade with Tyre (27:15), and the Apostle Paul stopped there on one of his journeys.

Cyprus

Cyprus, off the coast of Lebanon, is the third largest island in the Mediterranean. It was rich in natural resources, especially silver, copper, and lumber. Jewish colonies developed there in the period between the testaments, and Paul encountered more than one synagogue there during his first missionary journey (Acts 13:5). The Gospel gained an early foothold there.

The Nile River

The Nile is the world's longest river, extending about 4,160 miles. Nestled in a narrow valley, it was the lifestream of the great Egyptian civilizations: 96 percent of the population lived within 12 miles of the Nile. The Nile flooded annually, providing irrigation for growing crops in the otherwise arid desert.

The Jordan River

The Jordan originates 1,200 feet above sea level north of the Sea of Galilee, near Mount Hermon, and descends to the Dead Sea some 1,300 feet

The source of the Jordan River

below sea level. It is in a straight-line course of 120 miles. The river winds extensively for 135 miles in the 65-mile section from Galilee to the Dead Sea. The river descends quickly, has many rapids, and its current is strong.

Happenings at the Jordan

The Bible records many events in or near the Jordan. Jesus was baptized there, and the Israelites crossed it on miraculously dry ground when they entered Canaan. In Joshua's day, an altar of stones was set up there to commemorate the crossing. The Jordan formed a natural boundary between Israelite tribes on both sides; another altar was erected to testify that God was witness to the friendship between the two sets of tribes.

The Sea of Galilee

This sea is located about 685 feet below sea level. It is a beautiful deep blue sea, with rugged hills rising abruptly from its eastern and western shores, about 2,650 feet above the lake's surface. Its position below sea level and flank of high mountains on the east make it susceptible to severe weather changes and great storms, some of which we read about in the New Testament.

God's Delight

The beautiful harp-shaped Sea of Galilee is truly a wonder to behold. Its deep blue color, offset by the barren hills around it, gave rise to a rabbinic saying that "[the Lord] has created seven seas, but the Sea of Galilee is His delight."

The Red Sea

The Red Sea separates the Arabian Peninsula from Africa. At its northern end, its two branches define the Sinai Peninsula—the Gulf of Suez on the western side and the Gulf of Aqabah to the east. The term Red Sea comes from the Greek translation of a Hebrew term that probably means Sea of Reeds.

What Is the Sea of Reeds?

Many Bible versions indicate in marginal notes or in the Bible itself that the Red Sea was known as the Sea of Reeds. This is the most likely meaning of the Hebrew term. The most famous references to it are when the Israelites crossed it coming out of Egypt. These references probably refer to a northern extension of the Gulf of Suez or to a separate lake east of the Nile Delta.

St. Katherine's Monastery at the foot of Mt. Sinai

Mount Sinai: The Mountain of Moses

Mount Sinai, where the Israelites camped and Moses received the Ten Commandments, is somewhere in the Sinai Desert. Its exact location is disputed, but the traditional site is a rugged peak in the southern part of the Sinai Peninsula, called *Jebel Musa* (Arabic for "Mountain of Moses").

The Mediterranean Sea

Palestine forms the eastern coastline for the Mediterranean Sea, a sea that stretches about 2,200 miles to the west. It allowed for great maritime civilizations to arise, such as the Egyptian, Phoenician, Greek, and Roman. It is mentioned many times in the Bible, but the Israelites were not a seafaring people and there were few natural ports on the Palestinian coastline, so it did not play a major role in Israelite history.

The Sea of the Philistines: The Great Sea

The Mediterranean Sea had many names in the Old Testament. It was most often called the Great Sea, or simply the Sea. It also was called the Western Sea or the Sea of Joppa (Joppa was a port city). Once it was even called the Sea of the Philistines, since the Philistines lived on the coast in southwestern Canaan.

What Was Palestine?

Palestine is the term popularly used today to describe the land that the twelve tribes of Israel occupied during biblical times. Its name comes from the name *Philistine,* and in the Old Testament the term designates only their territory, *Philistia.* By New Testament times, *Palestina* was a broader term, the title of a recognized Roman province. Since then, it has been a popular title and has been used for 2,000 years. Even the British called this province Palestine in the early twentieth century.

What Was Canaan?

In many Old Testament passages, the term Canaan refers to all the lands west of the Jordan (see Genesis 12:5), and, as such, it is fairly close to Palestine in its broader usage. In some Old Testament passages, however, Canaan refers to the Mediterranean coastland, especially Phoenicia, north of Israel (see Genesis 10:19).

Phoenicia

Acts 21:2 mentions Paul setting sail from the Aegean for Phoenicia. This was the region covered essentially today by modern Lebanon—the coastal area north of Israel. Its principal cities in biblical times were Tyre and Sidon. The Phoenicians flourished in the first millennium B.C., especially as merchants and traders on the seas. They are usually referred to in the Old Testament as Tyrians, Sidonians, or Canaanites.

The Israelite "Destruction" of Canaan

In the popular mind, the Israelites invaded the land of Canaan and completely obliterated it with superior military force under Joshua. However, they only burned three cities: Jericho, Ai, and Hazor. Most of their conquests were accomplished by surprise attack or by God's miraculous intervention. Also, they left many Canaanites living in their territories, contrary to God's commands.

Hazor: Capital Place

Hazor was the largest city built in Palestine in the biblical period. Its huge mound accommodated up to 40,000 inhabitants. It especially flourished in the second millennium B.C. as a great Canaanite capital. Joshua 11:10 indicates that "Hazor formerly was the head of all those kingdoms," indicating its place as political hub in Canaan at the time.

Mizpah: Biblical Retreat Center

At least six places were named Mizpah in the Old Testament, but the most important was south of Bethel, near Gibeon in Benjaminite territory. Its major significance was as a religious retreat center in the days of Samuel. Samuel called for a great day of fasting, confession of sin, and renewal at Mizpah after the Ark of the Covenant was recovered from the Philistines.

Beth-shean: Imposing Mound

Beth-shean (or Beth-shan) was a city in the Jezreel Valley, south of the Sea of Galilee. It has been occupied almost continuously from prehistoric times until the present. The accumulated debris of successive occupations has built up a large, impressive mound more than 70 feet high. It is most prominent in the Bible as the place where the Philistines hung Saul's dead body on their city walls (1 Samuel 31:10).

What Was Babel?

This was the Hebrew name for Babylon. It comes from the Babylonian *bab-ili* "gate of god."

Interestingly, the story of the Tower of Babel relates the name to the Hebrew *balal* "to confuse," referring to when God confused the languages that people spoke. There is no linguistic connection between the two words, but the word play is an effective and arresting one.

The Great Ziggurat at Ur

A massive temple-tower (called a ziggurat) was built at Ur about when Abraham lived. It stood 70 feet high and had 3 levels. A temple to the moon god Nanna was at the top, and long staircases led to the first level. A temple to Ningal, Nanna's consort, was at the bottom. The remains of this ziggurat still stand, the best preserved of the many that were built in antiquity.

Bethel: House of God

The name *Bethel* means "house of God." It was a town 12 miles north of Jerusalem, and it had an honorable reputation in Israel's early history. Abraham offered a sacrifice there, and Jacob had his famous dream there. During the period of the judges, it was an important worship center.

Bethlehem: House of Bread

Bethlehem means "house of bread." It is mentioned several times in the Old Testament, most prominently as the city where David was from, but its major importance was as Jesus' birthplace. Many holy sites have sprung up in Bethlehem, although the authenticity of many of these sites is questionable.

Bethlehem and the Prophet Micah

The prophet Micah predicted Bethlehem's rise to prominence in a remarkable prophecy (Micah 5:2): "But you, O Bethlehem Ephrathah, who are little to be among the clans of Judah, from you shall come forth for me one who is to be ruler in Israel, whose origin is from of old, from ancient days."

Masada and Herod's Terrace Palace

Masada

Masada is one of the most spectacular sites in the Holy Land. The city is on the flat top of an almost inaccessible rock bluff that thrusts dramatically upward from the wilderness floor near the Dead Sea. It was a fortified Jewish community that began in the second century B.C. The Romans had a garrison there about A.D. 6 until 66, when the Jews revolted and took it over again.

Jewish Zealots at Masada

Jewish Zealots forcibly occupied Masada in A.D. 66, and supplied it to withstand a long siege. It was the last Jewish stronghold to fall to the Romans during the Jewish revolt of A.D. 66 to 73. The Romans besieged it for seven months and built a ramp up the western side, where they breached the wall with battering rams. The 960 occupants inside all took their lives (except for seven women and children) in a suicide pact, rather than surrender.

Megiddo: Strategic City

Megiddo was a major Canaanite and then Israelite city in the Jezreel Plain in north-central Israel. It was located at the juncture of three major trade routes, commanding the main pass between the Plain of Sharon and the Jezreel Valley. As a result, it was the site of many important battles in Israelite history. An ivory plaque shows a prince of Megiddo receiving tribute and prisoners.

Solomon's Walls

Solomon fortified the walls of Jerusalem, Hazor, Megiddo, and Gezer (1 Kings 9:15). Jerusalem's walls were rebuilt so many times that Solomon's contributions are not recoverable, but they do remain at the other three sites. Megiddo had casemate walls, which means they were double walls with earth-filled rooms between the walls.

Glacis: A Cool Refresher?

No, it is not a new type of ice cream. It was a huge, steeply sloping mound that was built against the city walls to prevent battering rams from moving into position and sappers from tunneling under the city walls. Enemies attempting to scale the glacis were easy prey for archers on the tops of the walls.

Caesarea and Joppa: Lone Seaports

The smooth Mediterranean coastline of Israel has few good port cities. The Bible mentions two: Joppa and Caesarea. Only Joppa was a natural port—it was a small port from which Jonah sailed. Caesarea (north of Joppa) was built into a major port in New Testament times, through which Paul traveled several times.

Caesarea: Jewel in Herod's Crown

King Herod the Great constructed a massive breakwater about 200 feet wide and 150 feet deep to create a protected harbor at Caesarea. Many of the enormous stones can still be seen underwater today, extending 150 feet out from the shore. The city itself was also impressive, with a fortress, walls, and many large public buildings.

Damascus

Damascus was the capital of an Aramean kingdom in the early second millennium B.C., which was mostly hostile to Israel. Its foreign policy was preoccupied with keeping mighty Assyria at bay. Several Israelite kings fought rulers of Damascus, including Solomon, Omri, and Ahab. Elisha the prophet went to Damascus once and uttered a prophecy correctly predicting Hazael's succession to the throne there.

Roman aqueduct at Caesarea

Tourist Sites in Damascus

Visitors to Damascus have many sacred sites to choose from, despite the doubtful authenticity of most of them. Tourists may visit Adam's Cave, the Cave of Blood (where Cain supposedly killed Abel), the Cavern of Gabriel, and Moses' Tomb. There is also a mosque with a Minaret of Jesus, where Muslim tradition holds that the "prophet Jesus" will return to fight the antichrist.

Susa: Political Capital of Persia

Susa was the main diplomatic and administrative capital of Persia, and the kings and their courts

spent winters there. It is mentioned in the books of
Daniel, Nehemiah, and especially in Esther as the
Persian capital. It had magnificent palaces and
fortifications. The Bible refers to it as "Susa the
capital" (Nehemiah 1:1; literally "the fortress").

Persepolis: Sacred Capital

In many ways, Persepolis was the most impressive of
the Persian capitals, but it did not have any
diplomatic or political function. Rather, its major
function was sacred. The kings and their courts
would leave Susa and go to Persepolis for the spring
New Year's festival, and delegations from all the
nations within the Persian Empire went to offer
tribute and reaffirm their loyalties.

The Royal Terrace of Persepolis

Persepolis was divided into the official royal city and
a residential section. The royal sector was built atop
a gigantic artificial terrace, measuring 1,485 feet by
1,155 feet, and 40 feet above the plain. It was all
linked to the nearby mountain by a system of cut
stone blocks and iron and lead pins.

The Apadana of Persepolis

The Apadana was a great square hall (30,000 square
feet) that had a roof that was held up by 72
columns, each 27 feet high, where the Persian kings
received visiting nobles. Two great stairways led up
to this hall, which were decorated with reliefs. One
side of the relief shows the royal court, with guards,
armies, and chariots. The other side pictured 23
delegations of foreign dignitaries loyal to Persia.

Antioch of Pisidia

The Bible mentions two cities named Antioch. One was in the mountainous region of south-central Asia Minor (or Turkey), in the region called Pisidia. The Apostle Paul helped establish a church there and he visited it again twice (Acts 14:21; 16:6). The peoples of Pisidia were fiercely independent, which caused trouble for foreign powers.

Antioch of Syria

Antioch of Syria was the capital of a flourishing Roman province and hub of the entire Roman Empire in the east. It was very important in the early church—it was the first church to send out missionaries (Acts 13:1–3: Paul and Barnabas). Also, it was here that followers of Jesus were first called Christians (Acts 11:26).

Samaria: Israelite Capital

Samaria was the capital of the northern kingdom of Israel after the days of Omri (about 880 B.C.). It reached its height of glory under Jeroboam II, a century later. Impressive remains of Omri's and Ahab's building project have been found, including a fine sample of the Israelite casemate city walls.

Jews and Samaritans

After the exile, relationships between Jews, who had gone into exile, and Samaritans, who had remained in the land, were not friendly. Conflict arose when the Temple was rebuilt, and also later, when the walls were rebuilt. In the New Testament period, Samaritans and Jews were very antagonistic toward

The Good Samaritan helps the injured Jew.

each other; this puts in sharper perspective Jesus'
parable of the Good Samaritan, who helped a
Jewish victim of an assault.

Samaria: Israelite to the Core

Samaria was one of the few cities built by Israelites, rather than taken over from the Canaanites. In 1 Kings 16:24, we find that Omri "bought the hill of Samaria from Shemer for two talents of silver; and he fortified the hill, and called the name of the city which he built, Samaria, after the name of Shemer, the owner of the hill."

Shechem: Later Samaritan Capital

Shechem was an important city at the foot of mounts Ebal and Gerizim, in central Israel. Abraham and Jacob visited it, and Joshua and the Israelites renewed their covenantal vows there. It was a prosperous city during the Israelite monarchy, and in late centuries before Christ it served as the capital city of the Samaritans.

Shechem: Sacred City

In the early second millennium B.C., Shechem was known in extrabiblical texts as "the people of the confederation," which was held together by a sacred treaty or covenant. Several temples and sacred precincts have been excavated, and an impressive sacred standing stone, dating to 1450–1150 B.C., still stands today. Judges 9:46 mentions a temple there dedicated to El-berith, "the god of the covenant."

Cities and Water Supplies

All cities were built near springs or near streams that did not dry up in the summer. In cities where the spring was outside the city walls, water channels and

Megiddo water tunnel

tunnels were built to bring the water into the city. This was important in case the city was attacked by enemies. The water system of ancient Jerusalem has been completely excavated and visitors can hike through the tunnel.

City Life

All ancient cities were very crowded. With the rise in a concentrated population, work could become specialized and many trades arose besides hunting and farming. Trade between cities and regions opened people's vistas to faraway places. Travelers and merchants went from city to city, so people often heard the news of places far away.

Means of Travel

For the most part, people walked in ancient times. Camels carried the heaviest burdens for merchant traders and others who traveled. Donkeys were useful because they were very surefooted, even in the mountains. Horses were mainly used in the army for pulling chariots, and mules were used by kings and the rich. Wagons and ox-carts were commonly used to carry baggage.

Traveling Distances

Traveling in caravans of camels and donkeys was common in biblical times. People walking on foot could cover about 15 miles a day. Donkey caravans could travel about 20 miles a day. Fully loaded camel caravans could cover 18 to 20 miles a day. A man riding a fast camel could travel much farther, up to 70 miles a day.

A Persian Pony Express

The Persian empire was far-flung, reaching to India in the east, Ethiopia in the south, and Turkey in the west. An efficient messenger system existed to send official decrees and letters throughout the empire. They were sent by mounted couriers on fast horses that were specially bred from the king's stud (Esther 8:10).

Straight Street

The only city street identified by name in the New Testament is "the street called Straight" in Damascus (Acts 9:11). This is where a man named Judas lived. Judas had hosted the Apostle Paul for three days after he had been blinded, before his conversion. This street still survives.

The Daughter of Zion

This term was used many times in the Bible as a synonym for Jerusalem and its inhabitants. Sometimes it referred just to the women of the city, but it also referred to the whole population. The plural term "daughters of X" (where X was a city name) was commonly used, and had the same connotation.

Spain: Paul's Dream Destination

In his letter to the church at Rome, the Apostle Paul stated that after he had visited Rome, he wanted to go on to Spain, at the western edge of the Mediterranean, to carry the Gospel there (Romans 15:24,28). He did reach Rome (Acts 28), but we do not know whether he ever reached

Spain. Christianity did find an early foothold in Spain, however.

Sparta: Jerusalem's Sister City?

Sparta was the capital of Laconia in southeastern Greece. Sparta is not mentioned in the Bible, but a Jewish tradition held that the Spartans and the Jews shared a common ancestry in Abraham (1 Maccabees 12:20). Friendly relations existed between the Spartans and Jews in the second century B.C.

Dalmatia: Home of the Firehouse Dog?

From 2 Timothy 4:10, we learn that Titus, one of Paul's companions, had left him to go to Dalmatia. This was a Roman district in what is today Eastern Europe. It is thought to be the original home of the dalmatian breed of dog, the white-with-black-spots firehouse dog.

The Decapolis

This was a region of ten cities south and east of the Sea of Galilee. They were Hellenistic (Greek) cities loosely associated with each other, and were relatively free of Roman control. Jesus spent some time in the Decapolis, but much more in the region of Galilee.

The Athenian Areopagus

This is a hill northwest of the better-known Acropolis in Athens. It was the site where murder cases were tried. The name also refers to the judicial council that met there at times. The Apostle Paul was taken there to be questioned

about his teachings of Jesus and the resurrection
(Acts 17).

Where Is Armageddon?

Revelation 16:16 states that Armageddon is a
Hebrew word, but no such word is actually found
in Hebrew. Many scholars think it stands for *har-
megiddo* "mountain of Megiddo." Megiddo was the
site of two decisive battles in the Old Testament
between Israelites and foreign forces, and it might
well have served as a symbol of the great final
struggle between the forces of good and evil.

Macedonia: Paul's First Stop in Europe

Macedonia was the first place in Europe that the
Gospel was preached. It was a region of northern
Greece, and was for many years an independent
kingdom. Its most glorious period came under
Alexander the Great and his father Philip in the
fourth century B.C. The Apostle Paul was moved to
preach there by a vision in which a Macedonian
man called him to come (Acts 16:9). Paul visited
many cities there, including Philippi, Thessalonica,
and Berea.

An Ancient Tel Aviv

The modern Israeli city of Tel Aviv gets its name
from the ancient Telabib, an unidentified city along
the River Chebar, the great irrigation channel near
Babylon. Ezekiel visited the exiles at Telabib
(Ezekiel 2:15). The Hebrew term means "hill of
corn," but the same name in Babylonian means
"mound of the flood."

Tel Megiddo